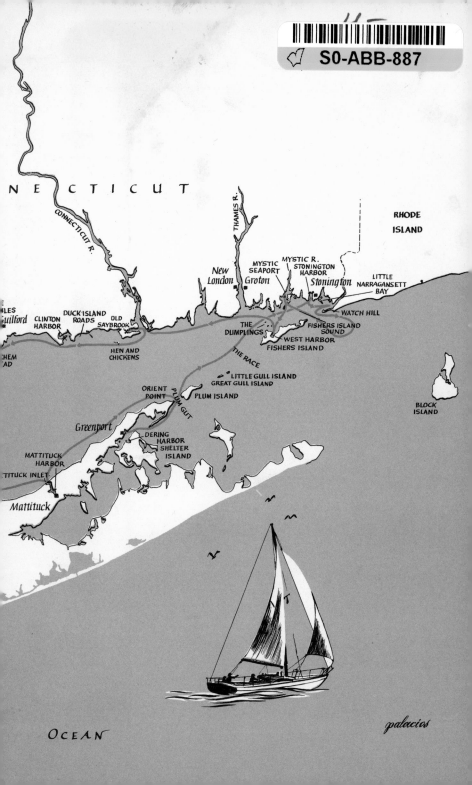

CONNECTICUT

CONNECTICUT R.

THAMES R.

RHODE ISLAND

New London

Groton

MYSTIC SEAPORT

MYSTIC R.
STONINGTON HARBOR

Stonington

LITTLE NARRAGANSETT BAY

WATCH HILL

LES
uilford

CLINTON HARBOR

DUCK ISLAND ROADS

OLD SAYBROOK

THE DUMPLINGS

FISHERS ISLAND SOUND

HEM
AD

HEN AND CHICKENS

WEST HARBOR
FISHERS ISLAND

THE RACE

LITTLE GULL ISLAND
GREAT GULL ISLAND

ORIENT POINT

PLUM GUT

PLUM ISLAND

BLOCK ISLAND

Greenport

DERING HARBOR
SHELTER ISLAND

MATTITUCK HARBOR

TITUCK INLET

Mattituck

OCEAN

palacies

THE INLAND SEA

BOOKS BY MORTON M. HUNT

THE NATURAL HISTORY OF LOVE

HER INFINITE VARIETY: *The American Woman as Lover, Mate and Rival*

MENTAL HOSPITAL

THE TALKING CURE *(with Rena Corman and Louis R. Ormont)*

THE THINKING ANIMAL: *A Report on the Rational and Emotional Life of Modern Man*

THE INLAND SEA

THE INLAND SEA
BY MORTON M. HUNT

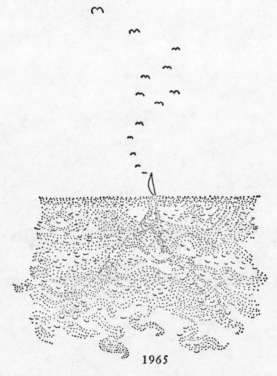

1965

DOUBLEDAY & COMPANY INC., GARDEN CITY, NEW YORK

The contents of this book originated, in somewhat different form, as a series of articles in *The New Yorker*.

AUTHOR'S NOTE

To see the world in a grain of sand is a more difficult feat than I care to attempt, but I *have* attempted here to see a good deal about modern America in that little Mediterranean Sea known as Long Island Sound. This book is neither a cruising guide, a narrative of personal heroism, nor a manual of small-boat handling; it is, rather, an effort to see in microcosm as much as I can about modern American life and the irreversible changes—some welcome, many regrettable—that it is making in the face of our earth.

Long Island Sound exhibits, in a mere hundred miles, many things: the ways in which Americans use and enjoy, misuse and destroy our most beautiful natural resources; the inexorable march of Progress, Growth, and Improvement, and the consequent homogenization of the countryside; a broad sampling of human activities, ranging from modern industry to sunning and swimming, and from nuclear submarine construction to clamming; and above all the contradictions within so many men today, which cause them to embrace all the benefits of contemporary society and yet to seek more energetically than ever to escape from it, at least temporarily, into the simplicity of sun, storm, and sea. For modern man is desperately in need of a means of self-renewal; and since we came out of the sea unthinkably long ago and still bear its traces in the very chemistry of our cellular fluids, it provides us with an ultimate refuge and an atavistic feeling of well-being.

My purposes, therefore, were several: to observe and report what I could learn about modern America from this hundred-mile cross-section of it; to experience for my own sake once again those natural beauties that are rapidly vanishing forever, in the area of the eastern megalopolis; and to transmit as well as I could the value I find in a rediscovery of the senses of the physical being I inhabit.

The cruise described herein was made late in the summer of 1963, and while a number of minor changes have occurred around the Sound since then, I have interrupted the narrative only once or twice to take note of them. One or two people have retired, several marinas have expanded, and nearly everywhere there is somewhat more activity and less tranquillity; other than that, the portrait is as accurate as I could make it.

It is always pleasant to thank those who have been of help in the making of a book. My good friend Albert Brown deserves thanks for having introduced me to sailing and taught me its rudiments, a dozen years ago, as well as for having been an invaluable assistant on the first part of the cruise described in this book. John R. Whiting, another old friend, also taught me a good deal about boats, and about Long Island Sound, and even entrusted to me his beloved new boat, *Merrywend*, on which I circumnavigated the Sound. William Shawn, the editor of *The New Yorker*, deserves my particular gratitude for having underwritten this project and for guiding it with the lightest and yet the surest of editorial touches. Robert Macmillan, also of *The New Yorker*, made innumerable helpful suggestions in the final stages of polishing the manuscript. I also owe thanks to my various crew members for having helped hoist sail, steer, swab the deck, navigate, and cook, but most of all for seeing things all about us with their own eyes and for transmitting to me some of their sense of wonder at it all.

Amagansett, Long Island
September 1964

6

THE INLAND SEA

THE ANCIENT ROMANS boastfully referred to the Mediterranean as Mare Nostrum, and if New Yorkers are not empire builders in the same sense, they, too, have a sea of their own. Long Island Sound may be just an elongated puddle by comparison—it measures no more than a hundred miles from one tapering end to the other and a mere twenty miles across at the widest part of its midriff, whereas the Mediterranean is over two thousand miles long and as much as a thousand miles wide—yet it has some remarkable similarities to the original Mare Nostrum, which was also often called Mare Internum in ancient times. The Sound is itself a mediterranean, or inland, sea, being almost entirely enclosed by land and yet composed of the same salt water as the Atlantic Ocean, with which, through a strait at its eastern end—and,

9

to a lesser extent, through the East River, at its western end—it exchanges huge quantities of water, micro-organisms, and fish at each flood and each ebb of the tide. Ocean water and life entering an inland sea in this fashion diffuse themselves through it, and the citizens of its dominant city similarly diffuse themselves upon its shores; Romans were scattered along both sides of the Mediterranean, from Carteia, in Hispania, to Gaza, in Palestine, and New Yorkers are comparably flung far along the edges of Long Island Sound, from Willets Point, in Queens, to Watch Hill, in Rhode Island.

The shores of the Mediterranean included many kinds of topography and were occupied by many peoples besides the Romans; the same thing, on a smaller scale, is true of the internal sea enclosed by New York and Connecticut. Its coastline is sometimes ragged, being sprinkled with islands and perforated with harbors, and at other times it is straight, naked, and incapable of affording shelter. Along the margins of the Sound, smoky seaports and pallid industrial towns alternate with fresh-faced fishing villages and wooded promontories. Hard by public beaches that are densely packed in summer with nearly naked human bodies rise mansions splendidly set off by lawns sloping unpeopled down to the water. Cockleshell dinghies sailed by bleached and tanned children frolic just offshore, while a mile or two farther out barge-hauling tugs shoulder their way purposefully along, leaving a stain of diesel smoke in the air.

A surprisingly broad range of American society is to be found beside, on, in, and under the waters of the inland sea. The poor come by bus to lie on beaches or to fish from public docks, the rich arrive by limousine to sit baronially on their patios or on the decks of their yachts. On a fine day in midsummer, something like a million people may wade or swim in the waters of the Sound, a couple of hundred thousand may float on top of it on anything from rubber rafts to three-masted schooners, and several hundred may be hidden within its turbid depths, whether in skin-diving gear or in the black hulls of nuclear submarines. A child will notice no more of the Sound than its glistening edge, all ooze and empty shells and cast-up jellyfish. An estate-owner looking out over his lawn to the water and the far shore beyond will see it as a spacious backdrop to his property and as a protection from the encroachments of the mob. A jet pilot descending from a crossing of the Atlantic will see it as a shallow, wrinkled inlet of the ocean that passes beneath him in fifteen minutes. The skipper of a small boat caught on it by a storm will view it as a vast ocean—shoreless, profound, and savagely bent on swallowing him up.

Much of this extraordinary diversity is rapidly being smoothed out. Promoters, builders, and developers are energetically attacking the more primitive parts of the coastline; powerboats and outboard motorboats are proliferating like pond scum, to fill the bays and harbors with noise and fumes on weekends; the once quiet mansions of the few are being turned into busy beach clubs for the many; and even the romantically treacherous strait at the eastern end of the Sound —called The Race, because of the mad rush of the tides through it—may eventually be reduced to humiliating insignificance by the erection of a bridge linking Orient Point and Watch Hill.

Though I have known the Sound intimately for only a dozen years, I have become sufficiently devoted to it to grieve over the changes that time will bring, as every lover despairs to think of the fading of his beloved's beauty. In order to experience the Sound in what remains of its variety, therefore, I decided to make a modest odyssey in the summer of 1963— a leisurely two-week trip around the Sound in a cruising sailboat. From a friend I chartered a year-old Medalist-class sloop named *Merrywend*, having ascertained that her hull was thirty-three feet long over-all and was made of fiber glass, that although her lines were not racy, she was trim and agreeably curved, and that there was plenty of deck space on her bow, a roomy cockpit aft, six bunks and a fully equipped galley and head below, and an inboard auxiliary motor. Then, unfolding charts on my bed at home in the city, I decided to circumnavigate Long Island Sound counterclockwise. From Stamford, where *Merrywend* was berthed, I would sail westward about twenty statute miles (in this account I will use the familiar statute, or land, mile, rather than the mariner's nautical mile) along the coast of the mainland as far as the Bronx; then eastward a hundred miles along the shores of Long Island to Orient Point and across The Race to Watch Hill, at the Rhode Island border; and, finally, westward again along the Connecticut coast for eighty-five miles, ending up back at Stamford. My notes of that trip, which follow, are not so much a ship's log as a journal of a two-week episode in an *affaire du coeur;* some day, when I am "old and grey and full of sleep, and nodding by the fire," perhaps I will reread them, and remember the Sound, how it was.

Friday, August 9

A VISITOR to any one of the yacht clubs, marinas, or town harbors rimming Long Island Sound by the score will, if he stands on the dock and looks about him, almost certainly be struck by the beatific expression on the faces of the people lugging supplies aboard their boats for weekend cruising. Though they may be having a hard struggle with cardboard cartons full of groceries, canvas tote bags, armloads of clothing, and large, recalcitrant chunks of ice, they seem to move in a cloud of the purest euphoria. A naïve observer would be likely to ascribe this to their anticipation of the delights of the trip, but I suspect that it is deeper-rooted—that the collecting and caching of food give rise to a primitive feeling of well-being, an ancient satisfaction at one's self-sufficiency and readiness to cope with hard times to come. This is particularly true when the caching of food takes place on board a boat, for once the sailor drops his mooring lines or hoists his anchor, he is cut off from the world of men and makes a world of his own, in which only his wits, his skill, and his carefully hoarded supplies keep him alive. At least, so it is in fantasy, and almost every man sailing across Long Island Sound feels himself to be another Joshua Slocum, capable of sailing around the world singlehanded.

Today, the first day of my cruise, dawned sunny, hot, and humid, and by the time I had hauled all the necessary armfuls of clothing, ice, and groceries from my car to the cockpit of *Merrywend*—a distance of about a city block along the piers of a big marina called Stamford Yacht Haven—I was dripping with sweat, though I was stripped to swimming trunks and canvas deck shoes. When it came to shifting the supplies below, to the main cabin—a small, bunk-filled compartment something like a Pullman drawing room—things got even hotter and stickier; nonetheless, I experienced a keen pleasure as I toiled away, stowing my clothing in drawers and a closet, and tucking cold cuts and other perishables in the icebox, cereals and cookies in the cupboard, and canned goods in little lockers under the main bunks. Blow, winds, and crack your cheeks! I thought; I shall lie snugly at anchor in some lonely inlet, heat my clam chowder and hot dogs on the alcohol stove, and dine content. Having finished these chores, I spent an hour checking over the boat from bow to stern to make sure I knew where all the essential gear was stowed; it is not only important but, again, very satisfying to know that the tools are in the first drawer under the radio table, the waterproof pullovers are in a cabinet next to the big closet, and various spare handles, blocks, lengths of wire, lubricants, and the like are in half a dozen compartments under the bunks.

Since it would be another hour or so before the arrival of my crew—an old friend named Al Brown and his seventeen-

13

year-old son, Geoffrey—I took a walk around the docks of Stamford Yacht Haven, sight-seeing. Though many Long Island Sound harbors have had docking facilities of sorts for many years, this kind of thing—the large marina, run by a profit-making corporation, rather than by a private club or a township—is quite new. Yacht Haven consists of a small cluster of stores and service buildings on the eastern side of East Branch, which is a dead-end canal at the inner end of Stamford Harbor, and seven long floating piers parallel to each other, which jut into an inlet protected by an earthen breakwater. On both sides of each pier, many little docks stick out at right angles, like the teeth of a comb, and near each dock, on its pier, are multiple electric-power and running-water connections ready for the boats, over three hundred of which regularly tie up at these docks. Yacht Haven is the largest marina on Long Island Sound and it is only five years old, but it is fully occupied, and is soon to be expanded to nearly double its present capacity. Much the same expansion and domestication of boating is taking place elsewhere around the Sound. Formerly, most boatowners would keep their vessels tied up to moorings in harbor waters that were supervised by town authorities or yacht clubs, and would get out to them and back to shore in rowboats or launches. Today, many of the smaller harbors in the Sound are so crowded that there is no room for additional moorings; moreover, many of the newer breed of boatowners want the garagelike convenience of being berthed in a dock rather than moored out in the middle of a harbor. Marinas not only offer them this but also pack several times as many boats into a given space as could be accommodated if the boats had to swing about on moorings. The net effect, however, is not portlike but suburban.

Yacht Haven, I could see, had a representation of the whole spectrum of pleasure craft to be found nowadays on the Sound. At one small pier there was a gaggle of tiny dinghies and rowboats, most of them fitted with attachments for outboard motors. At the docks of a couple of the larger piers were small open sailboats and powerboats of the sort designed to take their owners out for a day's racing or fishing, with lunch in a bag, a bucket in place of plumbing, and a tarpaulin as shelter in case of a downpour, such boats being both too short and too shallow to have living accommodations under their decks. Most of the boats at Yacht Haven, however, were thirty- or forty-foot cruising sailboats, like *Merrywend*, or, for those who preferred power, comparable cabin cruisers, with full living facilities—boats, in short, in which people could stay offshore for days at a time. When new, such craft cost anywhere from twenty thousand to forty thousand dollars, but if this price range makes them sound like playthings of the upper class, the truth is that most of them are owned by middle-class, family-oriented people who could not afford paid crews even if the boats were large enough to house them, and who try to do most of their own housekeeping. There is usually too much for just a man and his wife to do, though, and the marina—combining the functions of a handyman, a garage mechanic, a gas-station attendant, and a once-a-week scrubwoman—stands ready to wash, gas up, repair, paint, and generally help out; a few of the more effete marinas even send dock boys around to collect garbage and to deliver the Sunday papers.

The upper-class echelon of boats proved to have a few representatives at Yacht Haven. At Pier 5, where my own boat lay, I was impressed by *Susie*, a fat Chris-Craft cabin cruiser about fifty-five feet long; this is less than twice the length of my boat, of course, but then the amount of space inside a hull is proportional not to its length but, roughly, to the cube of it, and, compared to *Merrywend. Susie* looked like a floating apartment. A constant stream of water, accompanied by a muttering noise, came from a vent under the portholes low on the port side of the boat, and a young man in sailor whites who was energetically shining her chromium fittings told me that the boat's air-conditioner, plugged into a power outlet on the dock to keep her cool belowdecks, was responsible for this. *Susie* looked trifling, however, compared to *Florencia II*, a sixty-five-foot power yacht at the far end of Pier 5. She loomed so high above her dock that a movable flight of stairs had to be kept on hand for embarking and debarking. Her wheelhouse was a small boy's dream of delight, all gleaming handles, dials, and radio equipment, and she had a furnished saloon as big as many a Manhattan living room. Two servants —a man and a woman—were loading supplies aboard, and a uniformed captain moved about on obscure errands of preparation; he must certainly have had one or two deckhands, though they were not visible at the moment. Such a boat is worth close to half a million, and I wondered what sort of person could own such a vessel; when I got back to *Merrywend*, which now looked very puny and petit-bourgeois, I thumbed through *Lloyd's Register of American Yachts* and found that *Florencia II* belonged to Mrs. Florence Schick Gifford of Wilton, Connecticut. I took her middle name to be the answer to my question.

A little after 2 P.M., my crew arrived, in a flurry of greetings, duffelbags, and cameras. After they were installed—Al took a bunk in the main cabin with me, and Geoffrey chose one in the compartment under the foredeck—we started the motor, backed out, and puttered slowly down East Branch. Stamford Harbor opened out before us, a bay a mile wide, with low, wooded land embracing it on either side and two long breakwaters of rock guarding its mouth. A host of sailboats and powerboats were moored in the harbor, and in the center a series of red and black buoys marked a dredged channel; we headed down this avenue for the opening between the breakwaters, meanwhile hoisting the mainsail and jib, and then cutting the motor. The wind, very light and from the southwest, eased us out onto a broad, flat, almost glassy sea; keeping a southerly heading, we ghosted along for twenty minutes or so, putting about a mile behind us, in order to be able to clear Greenwich Point when we came about westward on the other tack.

The air, glaring and hazy, lay heavy on the water and the earth. At sea, one quickly becomes aware of what an imperfect kind of vision we have, the band of radiations to which our eyes respond being so readily obscured by moisture or dust suspended in the air; Long Island, a mere four miles away, was only a gray-green blur far off on the horizon, though on a clear day I would have been able to make out a crisp green shoreline, and even recognize a few landmarks. Stamford Harbor, a mile away now, and Greenwich Point, a thick loaf of wooded land less than a couple of miles to our right, were likewise smeary, pale, and unreal. Yet the haze was only accentuating an unreality and remoteness that everything land-based has when one is at sea. The houses and smokestacks of Stamford, on the horizon, were already alien. What cars were moving about there, and what men were working in offices and women shopping in supermarkets, were unseen, unknowable, and unimportant; the town, the shore, the whole land was a muted world we had left. Near shore, a tiny plume of white spray crawled across the water where someone, almost in that other world, was water-skiing behind a motorboat, and from a beach on Greenwich Point we could faintly hear the joyful shrieks of children and see them and their mothers as myriad dark specks against the sand.

Coming about onto the port tack, we headed for Greenwich Point; the wind picked up a bit, and the sky on the western horizon began to turn sullen and lead-colored, though overhead and in the east it remained bright and blue. Greenwich Point was agreeably wild, tree-covered, and uninhabited-looking; I was saddened by the thought that, being town property, it would shortly be subjected to the dubious benefits of full-scale improvements as a recreation area. Just west of it lies Captain Harbor, one of Long Island Sound's score of major harbors. (There are also several score minor ones, which can accommodate only quite small or shoal-draft boats.) It is a roughly oval bay about two and a half miles wide and a mile deep; on the seaward side a string of rocks and islands makes a very imperfect outer barrier, and on the landward side various inlets, coves, and river mouths attract boats of many sizes to roost, as eaves and deep windowsills attract city pigeons.

We tacked around Greenwich Point and sailed cautiously into an inlet inside it called Greenwich Cove—the easternmost of five smaller harbors within the perimeter of Captain Harbor. We kept the chart in hand and watched the buoys closely, in order to stay in water deep enough for *Merrywend*, which draws five feet. The cove, a broad one, looked hospitable, its water only faintly ruffled and invitingly blue-green, but the chart showed that, except in the very center, most of it was less than three feet deep at low tide and was strewn with hidden rocks and sand bars. Early explorers of Long Island Sound must have been uncommonly daring to venture into places like this, since they could have no idea what lay under the surface of the water; probably they tempered their daring with sweat, sending crews ahead in longboats to take soundings until they knew where they might venture to drop anchor. Whether the Dutch navigator Adriaen Block, who, in 1614, became the first European to sail through the Sound, took his ship, *Onrust*, into Greenwich Cove I don't know; I do know that the Coast and Geodetic Survey chart shows any of a dozen places where she might have come to grief, although she evidently did not.

Shallow or not, Greenwich Cove harbored a small forest of slender masts; a few large boats were moored in the center, and off toward the south there were a hundred or more little sailboats, plus a number of motorboats. Ringing the water was low green land, some of it marshy-looking, some beach-fringed, and some solid, manicured, and dominated by fine houses looking out over the harbor. Each of the four other sizable bays or inlets on the mainland side of Captain Harbor no doubt had a similar complement of boats, beaches, and estates; the border between sea and land, whenever it is well

18

protected and kindly, draws men irresistibly, and always has done so.

We came hard about, retrimmed our sails, and sailed close-hauled out of the cove toward some islands that lay a short distance to the west. First came Hen and Chickens, a scattering of sea-washed rocks on which gulls perched, smug and chesty. Wee Captain, several hundred yards beyond, was a mere scrubby lump of land, but Little Captain, a bit farther on, was a respectable islet, a fifth of a mile long, with a public beach, a pavilion, and a dock from which a plump white ferry named *Island Beach* was just setting out across Captain Harbor for Greenwich. Half a mile beyond Little Captain was Great Captain, which, with an area of seventeen acres, was worthy of being called a real island; from a distance it seemed desolate and romantic, what with wind-twisted trees, grass-topped sand dunes, and a lonely stone lighthouse, but as we approached, we could see, at the end opposite the lighthouse, a number of powerboats anchored off a sandy beach that was littered with beer cans and crumpled paper and on which people were eating, fishing, or just lounging about. We stayed a couple of hundred yards off, to avoid shoal water, but through my binoculars I could read signs that said MEMBERS ONLY, which, from the look of things, weren't having much effect. Great Captain Island has not always been as primitive as it looks now; there used to be a large gambling house on it, which ran full tilt through the nineteen-twenties but fared ill during the depression and then burned down in 1944. Today, the government owns a small piece of the island around the lighthouse, and the rest belongs to Aerotec Industries, a Greenwich aircraft-parts firm, which uses it as a recreation area for its employees and unsuccessfully tries to keep seaborne trespassers from invading it.

The islands and indentations of Captain Harbor are typical of the north shore of Long Island Sound. One or two hundred million years ago, what is now the coast of New York and Connecticut was a blanket of Cretaceous deposits laid down on a hard-rock base. Rivers and streams gradually eroded the blanket into a series of valleys and hills; then, aeons later, a slow sinking of the coastal belt, plus a rising of the sea level as the last Ice Age ended, allowed the waters of the Sound to enter the eroded areas, forming bays, estuaries, and semi-enclosed harbors, and making islands of stony hills that had withstood the weathering better. For such reasons, the mainland side of Long Island Sound has a consistently ragged and indented shoreline, with a hundred and twenty-six islands and countless rocks and rocky ledges, many of which are visible only at low tide. Long Island, in contrast, is a huge mass of sand, soil, and broken-off rock that was shoved along by glaciers and dumped on a low ridge; in consequence, it is practically without indentation for more than half its length, and has no offshore islands whatever.

A little after 5 P.M., having passed close by some of these quondam hills, whose valleys now lay a good twenty feet under water, we swung north and headed for Nun 2, a conical red buoy marking the beginning of the channel into Greenwich Harbor, which is one of the five large sheltered bays within Captain Harbor and lies about midway between its eastern and western ends. It was time to be getting in; the slate-gray clouds of a coming squall covered the western half of the sky, the wind was whipping up and heeling us over, and the sea was beginning to kick up in an unpleasant chop. Once we were close in, we started our motor, dropped and furled our sails, and, passing an impressive fleet of boats lying at moorings, approached the Indian Harbor Yacht Club—a handsome old white clubhouse with stately pillars, a veranda, and a green roof, perched on a point of land commanding the harbor. Having seen us in the channel, an attendant came out in an open launch; I asked him if there was a vacant mooring we could use for the night, and he directed us to one, out near the larger boats. We came up on it slowly, heading directly into the wind, and fished the cork float aboard with the boat-hook, hauled up the muddy hawser attached to it, and made the hawser fast to a massive cleat bolted to our foredeck. The wind was singing in the rigging now, and the boat was bucking in the waves, which rolled in from the direction of Great Captain, but we, being securely attached to a large block of concrete lying on the bottom of the harbor, could cut our motor with the same sense of relief one gets when a plane touches down on a runway. Rain swept toward us, pearling the surface of the water, and we scrambled below, broke out the whiskey, crackers, and cheese spreads, and fell happily onto the bunks in the main cabin, relishing the fact that the squall lashing the boat was unable to disturb us in our dry retreat.

Half an hour later, the squall had passed, leaving the sky fresh-washed and dripping from bits of scudding cloud. We changed into shore clothing and blew three blasts on our horn, whereupon the launch came out and ferried us to the club dock. The Indian Harbor Yacht Club, a venerable and well-to-do body in whose veins flows some of the bluer Greenwich blood, does not ordinarily let transients use its clubhouse, but a cousin of Al's was a member and had arranged guest privileges for us. The main lounge, a large, nicely furnished room, was empty except for a few well-dressed couples having cocktails. I asked a stiff-backed steward why things were so quiet on a Friday night, and, lifting an eyebrow at my ignorance, he explained that in August nearly every boatowner in the Indian Harbor Yacht Club was taking a vacation cruise to the eastern end of the Sound or to Maine, or even possibly to Bermuda. He eyed our sports attire and frostily informed us that if we wished to eat at the club, we would have to use the veranda, since ties were required in the indoor dining room. The would-be blueblood in me was gratified rather than irritated; most of the restaurants and yacht-club dining rooms along the Sound accept guests in sports shirts, and the Indian Harbor Yacht Club is one of the few holdouts for the more genteel tradition. I respected the gallantry of its stand, which was all the more admirable for being both outmoded and certain to be overcome by the foe in the future.

On the veranda, where only one other table was occupied, we had a peaceful drink and ordered steak *béarnaise*. It had just arrived when an attendant on the lawn below the veranda loudly rang a bell several times. Our neighbors on the veranda, and the people inside the clubhouse, got up at once and stood stiffly at attention, facing the lawn, and we, too, hastily scrambled to our feet likewise, feeling a trifle gauche. At the foot of the flagpole, the attendant knelt by a little brass cannon, from which in a moment there issued a startling *bam!* and a puff of dark smoke. Then he slowly lowered the flag, and when it was safe in his arms, the diners sat down and started talking again. Al chuckled at the ritual, but I scowled at him in reproof; for the moment, I would fain have been a Greenwich thoroughbred.

Saturday, August 10

SLEEPING AT ANCHOR is a very different experience from sleeping in a bed onshore. One keeps becoming half conscious of the slithering movements of the boat, the lapping of water against the hull, and the changing sounds of the wind—particularly on the first few nights of a cruise, before either the body or the mind is adjusted to life on a boat. Such sleep is like that of a cat—contented, luxurious, but instantly wakeful. This ancient animal mode of slumber, far from being unpleasant, is delicious and even sensuous; each half hour of sleep stolen between moments of awareness is savored greedily, and the waking to peep out a porthole and the falling asleep again are as sweet as the waking and sleeping of entwined weary lovers.

At 6:30 A.M., sunlight streamed into the cabin through the companionway hatch and woke us. The sky had a lacy film of cloud—it dissipated within an hour—and a pale half-moon lingered in the morning light. The air was a trifle chill, and the cockpit was dripping with dew; we wiped it dry, and ate, on deck, a breakfast of orange juice, heaps of scrambled eggs, bread and butter, strawberry preserves, and coffee. Merely stepping on board a boat seems to increase one's appetite two- or three-fold, and this passionate appetite more than offsets the limited variety of food available and the primitive methods of cooking it.

By eight-thirty, we had hoisted sail and slipped our mooring and were headed southwest through Captain Harbor and along the ragged, busy shoreline of Port Chester, Manursing Island, and Rye Playland. From a short distance out, the sailor would hardly think he was passing a solid phalanx of bedroom towns, for what he sees is merely a long, low green shore clothed in vegetation and dotted with fine homes set on classically rolling lawns, though occasionally he can spot a public beach, its pavilion flying bunting and pennants, or a little harbor chockablock with boats. Hidden behind this pleasant façade is the sprawl of suburbia, teeming with people; on this fine summer Saturday, we guessed, the attraction of sun and water must already have caused many thousands of these inland people to stir about and set forth on their weekend migration to the Sound. Indeed, we could see some of them appearing on the beaches, and both powerboats and sailboats were materializing on all sides and skimming past us with an air of determination on make-believe journeys.

It was an ideal day for boating—the air crisp and the wind brisk and steady from the northwest at about fifteen knots— and *Merrywend* boiled along, gently rising and falling, a creamy wash curling away from her bow and hissing as it slid by. The other boats on the water seemed equally happy;

23

the powerboats were bravely bouncing and kicking up sheets of spray, and the sailboats were gliding along heeled over romantically under the pressure of wind in their firm, full sails. For all our feeling of speed, we were probably doing no more than five knots (a trifle under six miles per hour), but then one beauty of sailing is that very little real movement gives the mariner the illusion of speed. The pleasantness of the illusion comes, perhaps, from the fact that the transporting of boat and people is wrung from wind and water by one's own skill. Or perhaps, as with chamber music, the heightened effect is due to economy of means; five knots achieved with two sails, two sheets, and one rudder seems far faster and surely more important than fifteen knots achieved with gasoline, sparkplugs, pistons, gears, and twin propellers.

The western end of Long Island Sound—that is, the eleven miles from Mamaroneck to Throgs Neck—tapers rapidly from a width of about five miles to a series of passages a mile wide or less, around and between various points and islands. This area has the Sound's highest density of population, the largest aggregation of boats, and the greatest frequency of summertime boat races. Already, as we approached Mamaroneck, one race seemed to be shaping up a mile or so offshore, and, deciding to take a closer look at it, we turned onto a southerly heading, so that the wind, on our starboard quarter, bowled us along in a rollicking kind of motion toward Matinicock Point, on Long Island, which was four miles away but as sharp and clear today as if it were four blocks away. To our right we could clearly see Manhattan rising out of the Sound, twenty miles away; the lower stories of the buildings and the island itself were hidden below the horizon of water, and would have been hidden by the Bronx as well, except that it, too, was hidden by the water, upon which the towers of the city floated like a mirage.

Halfway across the Sound, we drew close to the race; eight small day-sailers, each with a crew of three, were milling about near a large, anchored committee boat, from which, as we passed nearby, there suddenly came the dull crump of a five-minute warning gun, alerting the skippers to jockey for position near the starting line. The pure white sails, brightly colored hulls, and wary circling of the little boats contrasted oddly with the stolid look of a squat dark-green tug half a mile beyond them that was laboriously towing five loaded sand barges toward New York. The Sound, a playground to so many people, is a functional highway to bargemen and tugboatmen, and the frenzied activities of the racing skippers who scramble around under their bows must strike them as absurd. Tug and tanker captains pay little heed to races crossing their path and just lumber along, assuming that no one will be fool enough to insist on the right-of-way that a sailboat is legally supposed to have over any boat using power. Nearly always the captains are right, but the increasing amount of present-day racing appears to make this an increasingly risky assumption. The Coast Guard supervises about two hundred races a summer in this end of the Sound, and there are many hundreds of others, which need no supervision. Formerly, racing sailors were a small in-group of upper-class sportsmen; today thousands of businessmen, professional men, and the like race sailboats on the Sound, with their sons or daughters, and occasionally their wives, as crew. On weekday evenings during the summer, they touch up their boats, polish them, and minutely readjust their rigging—even half a twist on a turnbuckle that tightens or slackens a backstay may affect the straightness of the mast, and thus the pulling power of the mainsail—and on weekends they rise early, drive to the docks, and lug sailbags and other gear on board, ready for hours of work so strenuous as to allow no time for eating, drinking, or sight-seeing. In the summer, all over Westchester and southern Connecticut, many a Saturday-night party is dampened by the presence of sunburned men who, having had a gruelling day of racing, wilt like cut flowers at nine or ten o'clock and have to be taken home early by their wives.

Having crossed the Sound in a mere forty-five minutes, we

spun around at a flashing green buoy just off Matinicock Point and headed back toward Mamaroneck Harbor, on the mainland side. The boats of the race we had been watching were now remote and tiny, over close to the far shore; as we looked, blue-and-yellow spinnakers—light, parachute-shaped sails used when the wind is mostly astern—blossomed forth from one after another of them. The boats looked a brave and piratical lot as they bore down on us, and, unlike the tug captains, we prudently tacked away.

The *Merrywend* library includes a copy of Duncan and Blanchard's *A Cruising Guide to the New England Coast*, and from it I had learned that Mamaroneck Harbor has eight yacht clubs and seven boatyards, accommodating a total of twelve hundred boats, of all sizes, and is about the busiest small harbor on the Sound and a good place to acquire some notion of the boating boom of the nineteen-sixties. Recrossing the Sound at a brisk clip, heeled over smartly and sheeted in hard, we got to the broad outer harbor of Mamaroneck by noontime, and lowered sail and dropped anchor to have a peaceful lunch. The chart showed us that the inner harbor consisted of a kind of Y about a mile long, each arm of which had a channel with a turning basin at its tip. After lunch, we motored slowly into the lower part of the Y; on the shore to our left was a tall brick apartment building, and on the shore to our right was a turreted Victorian castle with a modern glass dining room built onto it and with cabañas on a beach below. In the channel, traffic was by now as heavy as it is on Sixth Avenue on Monday morning; boats puttered along in line, cabin cruisers sometimes honking their horns impatiently at slow sailboats. More boats were tied up along either side of the traffic lanes, and the people aboard watched the promenade of arriving and departing craft with the pointless but compulsive intensity of spectators at a fire. On one seedy old powerboat, a paunchy, red-faced Bacchus kept an eye out for strangers—easy to spot, since, like us, they were using charts to enter the harbor—and bellowed to each in turn, with a genial wave of his beer can, "O.K., Skipper, straight ahead! Straight ahead!"

The stem of the Y and both its arms being rather narrow, the harbor rules require each boat to be tied up fore and aft, with the bow pointing toward shore and the stern pointing outward, and both made fast to moorings, so it won't swing about with the wind and tide. In this way, hundreds of boats can be accommodated in a limited area. We motored slowly up the watery aisle between the ranks of boats of all sorts, marvelling at the efficient use of water space here. Onshore, yacht clubs sported umbrella-shaded tables, at which people were lunching or playing cards; scraps of beach were crowded with sunbathers; the gas docks of marinas were jammed with boats being serviced; and a few yards behind this maritime scene were private houses with washing hung out to dry. Everywhere, on shore, on the docks, and on the boats, were boatowners—tanned men and women, accompanied by an inordinate number of small children wearing bright-orange life jackets—all busy gassing up, stowing things, tinkering, putting sails on, starting motors, and shouting things like "Billy, hand me the sailbags next!" and "Muriel, for God's sake, never stand up in the dinghy!"

After examining both arms of the Y, we headed out of the harbor. Now, as we looked across the Sound toward Hempstead Harbor, five miles away, it appeared that hundreds of sails were touching each other all along the horizon, somewhere near the mouth of that harbor. This, of course, was an illusion, the result of foreshortening; the boats were actually spread out, but from our distance the spread was invisible, and one could scarcely see the shoreline for the sails.

For the next few hours, stripped to our shorts and baking in the sun, we proceeded rather languidly, in a dying wind, past Larchmont, New Rochelle, and the Bronx. The west side of City Island, our destination for the night, is only seven and a half miles from Mamaroneck Harbor, but the journey seemed very long, in part because the failing of the wind left us to idle haplessly in the heat, and in part because the shore-line here is so cut up by bays and inlets, and the water so strewn with islets, rocks, hidden reefs, and buoys, that we had to take a circuitous route. From offshore, this high-density strip of suburbia has a green and unspoiled look. Sand is a rarity on the mainland side of the Sound—at low tide most of the shoreline is mucky—and consequently there is nothing like the façade of hotels at Miami Beach or Atlantic City. Instead, one sees long stretches of gently rolling land that slopes down to a marshy or rocky shoreline. This makes for a picturesque look from a boat, with houses, trees, and even roads very close to the water's edge, and may help explain why the Sound, unlike Miami Beach and Atlantic City, appeals more to people who want to use the water actively than to those who prefer to lie oiled and indolent in beach chairs.

During the afternoon, I fell to wondering what it is that causes men to give certain geographical objects the names they do. Why, for instance, are so many little clusters of offshore rocks in the Sound, including the cluster we saw at the mouth of Captain Harbor and another that we now passed off Larch-mont, named Hen and Chickens? Duck and Ducklings would surely be more appropriate. In the next hour or so, we passed, among other landmarks, Umbrella Rock, which looked nothing like an umbrella; Horseshoe Harbor, which *was* shaped like a horseshoe; Table Rock, which was under water, and therefore not very tablelike; Hicks Ledge, with no nonsense about it, though I haven't any idea who Hicks was; and Middle Ground, another recurrent name, signifying a shoal or underwater ridge that rises toward or to the surface midway between the main-land and some other body of land. Along other stretches of the Sound there are names quaint enough to have been thought up by real-estate men; my favorites include Gangway Rock, Stepping Stones, East Nonations, Cow and Calves, the Dump-lings, Grassy Hammock Rocks, North Brother, Goshen Ledge, and Blackboys. Half the fun of cruising on the Sound would be gone if they were all reassigned sensible modern labels,

28

so that a skipper, instead of telling the helmsman, "Head for East Clump," had to say something like "Head for F-three-point-two."

One of the larger rocks we passed during the afternoon was a craggy mass called Pine Island, just off New Rochelle. Possibly foreshadowing the way things will look in an over-populated world, every flat spot on this inhospitable rock was covered with human bodies, perched on folding chairs or sprawled on blankets; the effect was reminiscent of one of those offshore rocks one often sees blanketed with sea birds. Through the binoculars I could read a sign on a small white shack atop the rock: NEW ROCHELLE ROWING CLUB. A number of the bird-people had cookstoves, lunch baskets, umbrellas, and other picnic gear crowded onto their few square yards of ledge, but from where we were it was not apparent whether they also rowed, or had boats of any kind; actually, as I happen to know, a handful of them do own racing sculls.

Just beyond Pine Island is Davenport Neck, a peninsula a little over a mile long lying mostly parallel to the shore and dotted with mansions in Georgian, Victorian, and nineteen-twenties-modern style. Each of them has a lawn and a beach, and, as we sailed past, we noted that these were well sprinkled with bathhouses, cabañas, umbrellas, and hundreds of people. From a quarter mile offshore we could hear amplified music, the whistles of lifeguards warning children to stay in bounds, and an occasional announcement, such as "Doctor Davis . . . Doctor Davis . . . Come to the office, please." The former owners of these mansions had sold them and fled farther east, leaving their homes to be converted into beach clubs. Possibly by the time my unborn grandchildren can sail, the whole shoreline of the Sound will serve the Greatest Good of the Greatest Number, but I am not quite enthusiastic about the prospect.

We were now passing among a number of islands, ranging from mere rocks to fairly large pieces of real estate, such as Glen Island, of nineteen-thirties dance-band fame (it is now a recreation area), Davids Island (occupied by an eighty-acre military establishment called Fort Slocum, which is currently used as a training school for Army public-information officers), and, to the southwest, the long twin shapes of City Island and Hart Island, about half a mile apart. On our right as we headed down the passage between them we could see the smooth curve of Orchard Beach (City Island lies immediately to the south of it), and it looked much like Coney Island—thickly covered with tens of thousands of people, who had come there by subway and bus. Across the water drifted the attenuated, piping cries of children and the high-pitched screeches of women. Orchard Beach is part of a peninsula that is now known as Rodman Neck, but was formerly called Anne's Neck, in honor of the dissident Puritan Anne Hutchinson, who settled here in 1642 with several fellow-refugees from Massachusetts. I could not help wondering how Anne would have felt about all these thousands of semi-naked hedonists on the shore of her settlement.

This part of Long Island Sound, so close to the city, is much more than just a playground for New Yorkers. On islands to both the right and left of us, for instance, we saw steel antenna towers for the transmitters of major radio stations in the metropolitan area. On Hart Island, a bleak piece of relatively undeveloped land, were a tall smokestack and a group of prison buildings—a city workhouse for fourteen hundred short-term offenders. A mile away, right in the middle of a procession of powerboats and sailboats, a huge empty tanker named *Poling Bros. No. 1* plowed sturdily along toward the East River and the Brooklyn docks, where it would be filled with oil for New Haven or Bridgeport.

City Island proved to be the biggest and busiest island we had seen all day—a mile long, tree-shaded, dotted with houses, bristling with piers, and completely surrounded by swarms of boats of every size and shape. Though it still looks tranquil and lovely from the water, it has undergone great changes in the past fifteen or twenty years. Before the war, it was the major center on the Sound for the building, repairing, and mooring of huge private yachts. Most of the people who lived on City Island then—and there were several thousand of them —devoted themselves to taking care of the yachts and their owners, and the island had somewhat the atmosphere of Martha's Vineyard or Nantucket. Today, the boating boom and the growth of the city's population have driven the great yachts eastward, and the shipyards of City Island build only a few of the larger yachts for the wealthy but peddle numbers of little fiber glass day-sailers and powerboats for the middle class. The main street has become a row of frozen-custard stands, clam bars, bait-and-tackle stores, and marinas specializing in outboard rentals for fishermen. As we sailed around City Island, we saw none of this, but we did see that the former Nevins Boatyard, which was once probably the finest on the Sound, had closed down and been replaced by a gasoline dock; I had, moreover, heard from a friend that apartment houses would shortly be built on the site of the yard. Even more significant, I thought, was the fact that the waters we were sailing through, where the sumptuous yachts of the Morgans, Vanderbilts, and Huttons had formerly been moored, now contained a scattering of small sailboats and powerboats, plus a little white houseboat with an orange roof, pink print curtains in the windows, and a glass-and-aluminum front door.

A long pier juts out from the southern tip of the island, and this afternoon it was jammed with fishermen, chiefly Negro or Puerto Rican, who, it appeared, could afford the trip to City Island but could not afford to rent a fishing boat once they got here. One of them threw an empty beer can into the water, and Al and I speculated on whether the sticky black bottom of the Sound between City Island and Great Neck, a mile and a quarter across the water, was yet entirely covered with empty cans; the traffic here is so thick and the human use of the water so intense that the speculation is not unreasonable. Even the movement of the water—the water, that is, stretching anywhere from a mile to three miles in different directions from the southern tip of City Island—can be profoundly changed by the movement of men upon it; this whole expanse often gets so stirred up by the hundreds of powerboats charging back and forth over it that the surface, from shore to shore, becomes roiled in unnatural patterns. On a glassy sea, the wake of even a medium-sized motorboat will travel for miles; when hundreds of wakes are produced within confines like these, they travel, intersect, and tangle, resulting in an agitation of the entire mass of water, on which boats move with an uncertain, irregular lurching motion. Not many years ago, this phenomenon could be seen only in small harbors, but nowadays the whole broad stretch of water from Throgs Neck to Sands Point, including all of Eastchester Bay, Little Neck Bay, City Island Harbor, and Manhasset Bay, is unnatural, neurotic, and difficult to sail upon every weekend all summer long. Wallowing and bouncing, we sailed as best we could around the tip of City Island and through the hundreds upon hundreds of boats moored on its west side. By five o'clock, we were tied up at a guest mooring of the City Island Yacht Club, but even here the roiled water kept our boat moving uncertainly under us, and not until sunset had sent the powerboats home did the surface slowly calm down and resume its normal behavior.

The City Island Yacht Club, which we visited after having dinner in a restaurant on the main street, is a square, gray-shingled building, much more informal than the Indian Harbor clubhouse. A group of teen-agers in chinos or denims were whooping it up in the bar over soft drinks, and in the dining room, a rather sparsely furnished chamber where a couple of dozen adults were having dinner, sweaters, sports shirts, and Bermuda shorts seemed to be the uniform of the day. The steward introduced us to Dr. Woldemar Weiss, a ruddy, blond, middle-aged osteopath from Montclair, New Jersey, who is one of the directors of the club. Over a brandy, Dr. Weiss told us that the members come from quite a wide area, including much of Westchester County and northern New Jersey as well as New York City. "We're primarily a serious racing and sailing club," he explained proudly. "Out of a hundred and four boats owned by our members, only about ten are powerboats. Our members do a lot of their own work on their boats. They save money that way, and, besides, they're the kind of people who like to do their own work. We've got everything here from ten-foot frost-biters, for winter racing, to fifty-foot yawls, and at least four or five of our boats always enter the Bermuda Race." He called our attention to a slender crew-cut man crossing the room. "That's John Van Sant," he said, and went on, "Let me give you an idea how serious we are about our sailing. John told me the other day that he figures that in the last fifteen years he's driven seventy-five *thousand* miles between here and Philadelphia, where he lives, to sail seventy-five *hundred* miles in the Sound. The Philadelphia rivers don't give real room for sailing, and Chesapeake Bay just hasn't got the variety and beauty and genuine sea feeling of the Sound. There simply isn't anything else quite like it in the East—or maybe anywhere on earth."

Sunday, August 11

LONG ISLAND SOUND begins where the East River joins it—at the narrow passage between Throgs Neck, in the Bronx, and Willets Point, in Queens. From where we lay at City Island, we could see this passage about two miles south of us, with the graceful Throgs Neck Bridge, silvered by the morning sun, hanging over it. Our first order of business today was to touch base there before turning eastward. The

morning was bright and calm, and we sailed slowly across
Eastchester Bay toward Cherry Tree Point and Bronx Beach.
The Bronx at this point shows not a deceptively handsome
face, as at Rodman Neck, but its own homely one. Right down
to the water's edge crowd a jumble of brick apartment buildings, drab wooden houses, and dilapidated wooden fences and
sea walls; the "beach" along much of this shore is nothing
more than a brown mud flat. At the time we sailed past, a
rabble of powerboats filled a small harbor on whose stone
breakwater someone had dumped a rusting blue truck body,
and faded flags fluttered over a peeling pavilion at a public
beach.

The bridge itself looked as though it sought to escape from
all this. It begins its climb at Locust Point, near the base of
Throgs Neck, veering out a short distance over the water on
slender stilts, in a clean flight of roadway, and then curving
back high over the very tip of Throgs Neck before jumping
off its stilts and launching out over the East River on its
cables. As we sailed past the end of Throgs Neck, we stared
up at the bridge, which soars almost directly over the old
crenellated walls of Fort Schuyler. The fort once guarded the
approaches to the East River and Manhattan, but the apertures
for its cannon have been vacant for many years now. At the
very tip of Throgs Neck, a white house covered with ginger-
bread trim, in which a lighthouse keeper once lived with his
wife, stands next to a sixty-four-foot steel tower bearing an
automatic flashing red navigation beacon, which is what made
him obsolete. Behind the house and the beacon, and within
the old battlements, is an assortment of buildings; they were
once the barracks and armory of the fort, and are now the
Maritime College of the State University of New York. The
old order changeth, yielding place to new, and I am discon-
certed to find that I do not welcome it.

Having leaped off at Throgs Neck, the bridge arches across
the water for a mile to land in Beechhurst, Queens, between
Cryders Point and Willets Point. We sailed under it briefly;

34

ahead of us, toward the city, the air was a pale grayish brown, and behind us, toward the east, it was a pure and flawless blue. We came about and headed eastward, beginning our hundred-mile trip to the other end of the Sound. To our right lay Little Neck Bay, ringed by streets, a parkway, and the close-ranked houses of Bayside, Douglaston, and Village Park. At the inner end of the bay, in an anchorage too shallow for a boat like ours, a horde of powerboats and some small centerboard sail-boats were moored; from a couple of miles away, and with the houses as a background, this anchorage resembled nothing so much as a parking lot full of cars. On the eastern shore of the bay, in the Great Neck area, a few stubborn rear-guard estates could still be seen, but it is only a matter of time before they, too, yield to the inexorable thrust of the expanding suburbs.

It was getting on toward eleven o'clock of a fine Sunday morning as we passed close by Kings Point, a spur at the western end of the broad peninsula of Great Neck, and the boating boom started to manifest itself again. Ahead of us, the horizon from Larchmont, on the mainland side, to the mouth of Hempstead Harbor, on the Long Island side, was becoming uniformly dotted with white sails, and all around us, in the mile and a quarter of water between Great Neck and City Island, a steady stream of powerboats churned eastward down the Sound for the day, their motors roaring, their bows hiked way up in the air, their owners proudly watching the fans of spray curve off to either side. The insouciance of these boats and their skippers brought to mind an item I had clipped from the *Times's* boating page earlier in the season, about how many boats come to grief around here. In these waters stands Stepping Stones Light Station, a bright-red Victorian build-ing perched on a rock halfway between City Island and Elm Point, in Great Neck, and southeast of it for quite some distance stretches a shoal, in which there are a number of smaller rocks, marked by buoys and also clearly shown on the Coast and Geodetic Survey charts. Powerboaters, however, often come to the water not as mariners but as converted

Sunday drivers, and instead of buying and using proper charts, many of them rely on little gasoline-company charts (which carry an express warning that they are not detailed enough for navigational purposes), a few consult the little sketch maps in railroad timetables, and some merely search the waters ahead of them with their eyes. The *Times* reported that each summer, as a result, between seventy-five and a hundred boats—nearly all of them powerboats—grind onto the shallows or crunch upon the rocks of the Stepping Stones, and either sink on the spot or limp away.

Powerboating can be an elegantly executed sport, of course, but much of its recent growth has had little to do with either sport or elegance. John Scott-Paine, a lean, good-looking young man who runs Stamford Yacht Haven, had told me that in his opinion the growth of powerboating in the last few years has had very little to do with a love of the water. Many boatowners, he said, find merely owning their boats and showing them to friends preferable to using them on the Sound. If I wanted to see this phenomenon in full bloom, he added, I should by all means visit the Club Capri, a marina in Manhasset Bay, which is the body of water on the eastern side of Great Neck. Now, with this in mind, we rounded Hewlett Point, on Great Neck, and headed into Manhasset Bay, which is about three miles long and rather narrow and winding, and which at first glance we thought fairly undeveloped, for there was nothing in sight but occasional large houses scattered along a wooded sandy shore. When we pushed a little farther down it, however, we could see, beyond a sandspit on our left, a wider part of the bay, where Manorhaven and Port Washington squat down by the water, and where, from a distance, marinas and fleets of moored boats conveyed the impression of a classic busy harbor. From far off the sight gladdened us, but then we came upon something that warned us not to expect this port to be classic. The something was a small barge with a store on it—it looked like a houseboat—moored in the middle of the harbor; colored pennants flapped from halyards running to the top of a short mast, the doors were beach-house jalousies, and signs above the cabin proclaimed the vessel to be *Capn's Galley*. Two powerboats were tied up alongside and their occupants were ordering snacks or lunch. We dropped sail, motored up, and hove a line to an attendant, who, in return, handed us a menu offering soft drinks, sandwiches, French fries, shrimp, a "He-Man's Fried Seafood Plate," and ice cream. We bought some ice cream and shoved off. A short distance farther on was a second and somewhat larger float, whose sign read GULF MARINE SERVICE STATION. It had gasoline and diesel-oil pumps on deck, and here, too, a couple of boats were tied up alongside while their wants were attended to. The logical extension of this seemed plain enough: the floating drugstore may be next, the floating haberdasher will follow, and at last, inevitably, there will come the sail-in movie.

We motored on toward shore, where two marinas and a yacht club made a splendid clutter of docks and boats. As we came closer, a sign on one of the marinas identified it as the Club Capri. We pulled up at its outermost dock, and a dock-master assigned us to a space where we could lie tied up for several hours. The Capri is laid out with one wide central pier, which extends straight out from the land, and from which a number of large crossarms branch off. Along each crossarm are enough slips to berth dozens of boats. Either to help the boatowners find their way or simply to contribute to the décor, the crossarms have street signs, bearing such names as Bahama East and Bahama West, Tahiti East and Tahiti West. At the landward end of the central pier is a small white fake lighthouse; this is the head dockmaster's office and the control center for a public-address system over which people can be summoned from their boats to take phone calls or meet friends. As we stood on the pier staring at all this in some astonishment, a gay little awning-topped electric surrey trundled past us, carrying two women and a heap of luggage

37

to a large diesel yacht; at the Capri, evidently, one need not perspiringly manhandle one's stores aboard.

The boats in the slips at the Capri ran the gamut from plain (very few), through middling fancy (very many), to splendid (a good sprinkling). Nearly all were power cruisers, the chief exceptions being a few sailboats, a two-story houseboat with geraniums growing in window boxes, and a hydrofoil passenger boat, *Albatross*, which carries commuters from the Capri to Wall Street every weekday morning. All in all, the Capri had a collection of vessels quite different from what we had seen in any harbor we had seen thus far. And the people were even less typical as examples of boatowners and mariners. A few were wearing nautical clothing—denims, T shirts, canvas caps, and rubber-soled deck shoes—but the majority were dressed more in country-club or seashore-resort style, the women got up in toreador pants and silk blouses, with full makeup and teased hairdos, and tripping along on spike heels that occasionally got caught between the planks of the pier, and the men resplendent in flowered sports shirts and Bermuda shorts.

The three of us went exploring, to see what else we could see. Near the shore end of the central pier was Barge Inn, which had gone to sleep an old sand barge and awakened to find itself a small restaurant with a dance floor. Across the pier from it was a store in which the Capri mariner could buy charming but not waterproof foul-weather clothing, red carpets lettered "Welcome Aboard," and similar allegedly nautical equipment. On the shore, a palisade enclosed a large free-form swimming pool ringed with tables and chairs; at one side was a pink building with showers and dressing rooms inside it and a stage and dance floor outside it. A sizable complement of children swam in the pool while their mothers watched and gossiped.

Seated at one of the tables, in the shade of a tree, was the manager of the marina, a motherly, blondish woman in a flowered dress named Mrs. Alice Weitemeyer. The Capri, she told us, had been greatly enlarged and modernized six years ago, and could accommodate two hundred and thirty-two vessels, nine tenths of which, ordinarily, were powerboats. "We have a lovely group here," she said. "They're very social. They like dances and parties and charcoal cooking on shore. As you can hear, we pipe hi-fi into the pool area all day, but Saturday nights we have a live combo here, and a buffet party. At midnight, the combo moves into Barge Inn, and the livelier folks keep going till two or three o'clock. Most of our people are from New York, Great Neck, or Port Washington, but we also get transients in here from all over. Some of our boats travel down to Florida in the winter, but most of our people stick close to home. In fact, quite a few of them don't leave their slips very often. They just enjoy being right here." Somewhat bemused by this last point, we thanked her, and resumed our walk around the docks.

After a while, the three of us split up for a couple of hours. I looked things over and struck up conversations with Capri clients; most boatowners—even those who are customarily churlish on land—are congenial and talkative around their boats, and these boatowners, I found, were no exception. Some of them invited me on board, and I saw a variety of interiors, all a good deal roomier and more mechanized and electrified than anything you'd find in a sailboat like *Merrywend*. Many of the power cruisers, I noticed, tended toward land-based décor, including bric-a-brac, ashtrays on the tables, and television sets. I asked one man how all these things stayed put in a boat, and he reminded me that a powerboat does not heel over; moreover, he said, when a storm is coming, most powerboaters run for shelter, and since they have a speed of fifteen or twenty knots, they can usually get off the Sound before the storm catches them.

One boat that seemed particularly comfortable was a good-sized white-and-chromium Chris-Craft Constellation, built in 1961. A husky, pink-faced man in his forties, wearing shorts and a T shirt, was loafing on the rear deck, and when I introduced myself and asked if I might look at his boat, he said he would be delighted to show me around. The boat, he told me, had everything that he and his wife—who was sunning herself on the foredeck—could want; it was a real floating home. The saloon, which he showed me first, was carpeted in gold from wall to wall and had gold-and-beige-upholstered furniture; there was also a television set, a cocktail table, a liquor cabinet, and a gateleg dining table. The master state-room, forward, was also carpeted in gold; it had twin beds (not bunks), a vanity, a chest of drawers, two large closets, two electric heaters, and a bathroom with a stall shower, and, in fact, was indistinguishable from a room in one of the better motels. The wheelhouse, aft of and above the saloon, was a marvel of chrome handles, buttons, and dials; from this van-tage point the skipper could operate twin engines totalling five hundred and fifty horsepower, with which he could cruise comfortably at twenty knots or achieve a top speed of about twenty-five. Cruising in such a boat burns up twenty-five gallons of gasoline an hour, my host observed, and I could see why marina owners tend to prefer powerboaters to sail-boaters, for when a boatowner like my host comes in after a five-hour day on the water, he buys anywhere from forty-five to sixty dollars' worth of gasoline, while a sailboat skipper buys none, or perhaps a dollar's worth. "It's expensive," my host said, sinking down into a club chair in the saloon. "But I like to get somewhere. I started out with a small sailboat eight years ago, and switched to power almost at once. This is my fourth boat. Each one has been larger and faster than the last one, but this is also the most comfortable. It's a real home for us away from our apartment. We live in Cryder House, next to the Throgs Neck Bridge, but all summer long we like to run down here in the evenings and sit on deck and smoke and talk to our neighbors, or watch television. We take her out on weekends. On a typical Saturday, we might run out along the Long Island side to Huntington Bay, then cross over to Con-necticut and come back to Greenwich in time to have lunch at

40

Greenwich Harbor Inn and visit with people we know there. Then, in the afternoon, we might spend a couple hours cruising up or down along the Connecticut side, and then cut across to Cold Spring Harbor and dress up to have dinner at the Mooring. Then back here in the evening. We use the boat primarily as a means of transportation to different eating places, although sometimes on a weekend we'll go a few hours away and stay overnight in another marina. Sailboat people are completely different. They're more sea-going and sea-thinking; they're not home-away-from-home people. I've never yet seen a sailboat type come down in the late afternoon, as I often do, just to sit on deck and talk. A powerboat owner—" He was interrupted by the ringing of a telephone on the cocktail table—not a ship-to-shore phone but an ordinary, land-based instrument. He answered, and called his wife to the phone, and then he and I went on deck. "That's my daughter, calling from camp," he said. "I like having a phone handy here. I have a line running out to my slip and a jack-plug arrangement, so that when I'm tied up here, I can plug in the phone and anyone can reach me, same as if I were at home."

Shortly after leaving the powerboat, I ran into a sailing acquaintance I'll call Myron Collins. I had met Collins in a little Connecticut harbor early in the summer, and since he is a rabid sailboat type, I was surprised to see him here. He invited me aboard his boat for a cold beer, and explained that he berths it in the Capri for convenience, even though the marina is a strange place for a true lover of boating. "It's full of kids, dogs, organized play groups, dances, and barbecues," he said. "Also, there are always some real swinging boats, where they go for guitar playing and singing and drinking and so on. Or so I hear. But mostly this is a family sort of place. It's partly suburbia, partly a night club, and partly a wet country club. What it *isn't* is a yacht club. These people think of their boats as summer homes. Hell, I knew one fellow—an engineer—who had a thirty-five-foot power cruiser here two years ago and kept her tied down all summer. He'd run up the engines once in a while, and he even went out into the bay a couple of times, but he didn't try to go out on the Sound until the end of the summer, and then, when he got to the mouth of the bay, he saw a few whitecaps outside, so he came right back. As for the women around here, most of them love sitting on deck in nice clothes and looking chic, but they hate to go out, especially if there's any kind of a little chop."

I asked Collins why he himself wasn't out sailing today.

"On a sunny Sunday afternoon like this, you can't really sail anywhere within a couple hours of here," he said. "The water gets all torn up by the powerboats. You have to leave very early to get far enough away, and I couldn't do that today. Sometimes it makes me sad. I think maybe ours is the last generation that will be able to sail close to New York City."

When we left the Capri, around three-thirty, we found all of Manhasset Bay and the Sound outside it in a turmoil worse than anything we had felt yesterday off City Island. The boat wallowed and staggered along in a most disagreeable way, yet hundreds upon hundreds of sailboat men were making the best of it, and the horizon over toward Larchmont once again seemed to be made up of innumerable sails touching or overlapping. Just how many boats are based on the Sound nowadays is not certain, but the Coast Guard puts the summertime total, including small craft, at about two hundred thousand. This represents a tremendous increase in the past dozen years, and as a consequence of it the mores of cruising are undergoing necessary revisions. A decade ago, when I first sailed on the Sound, it was the usual practice to drop one's garbage overboard as soon as the boat was well offshore. Today, with such hordes of people on the water, even the hundred-mile-long Sound would become a littered mess if everyone did that, and the Coast Guard has been repeatedly warning one and all that it is a federal offense to throw garbage or other trash anywhere in United States territorial waters.

Even so, the western end of the Sound is strewn at the close of each summer weekend with paper cups, floating beer cans, paper plates, melon rinds, and an indeterminate jetsam that is sometimes collected by eddying currents into streaks and patches of muddy scum. A brisk wind will charitably hide it, making the surface of the water look fresh and clean, but when the wind dies, it reappears. Swimming off one's boat is no longer a simple matter; one must search carefully for clean water.

The torn-up surface, combined with a failing wind, made the motion of our boat so inefficient that we started our motor off Sands Point without dropping sail. In this fashion, we ambled along for the next fifteen miles and three hours, passing Manhasset Neck, crossing the wide mouth of Hempstead Harbor, and paralleling Glen Cove, Matinicock Point, and, farther on, a gently curving shoreline of lawns, woods, and scattered houses, which extended to Rocky Point, on the near side of the mouth of Oyster Bay.

Oyster Bay and Cold Spring Harbor, its continuation, together form a narrow, carrot-shaped body of water reaching four and a half miles into Long Island. About a third of the way from the mouth of Oyster Bay to the inner end of Cold Spring Harbor, a passage bears off to the west, widens out, and winds around to the right like a fat snail. The first half of this snail is called Oyster Bay Harbor, and it affords excellent shelter and fairly navigable water; at its outer end is the very posh and exclusive Seawanhaka-Corinthian Yacht Club, and at its inner end is the busy little port of Oyster Bay, accommodating a fleet of pleasure craft, a flotilla of oyster dredges, and a fair-sized shipyard. The shoreline on both sides of the curving length of Oyster Bay Harbor consists of low-lying green-clad hills; scattered houses appear through the trees, and the town of Oyster Bay is a picture-postcard assemblage of roofs, chimneys, and spires. We hastened past all this, for our objective was the second half of the snail—a landlocked basin around to the right, behind a peninsula inaccurately called Centre Island. On my charts, the basin, which is about two miles long and a mile wide, has no name of its own, but local people often call it Morris Cove. It is entered from the south; on the other three sides it is enclosed by land, though the northern boundary is only a low, scrubby sandspit, on the other side of which is Long Island Sound.

To get into Morris Cove was a fair amount of bother, involving a five-mile trip from the mouth of Oyster Bay, but the Cove proved worth it, simply by way of contrast to the Capri. Here we were amazingly apart from everything improved, civilized, comfortable, and crowded. Almost all around the oval basin is a wooded shoreline, with occasional stretches of lawn and a large house or two. We dropped anchor on the eastern side, near Centre Island—a hundred yards from a stretch of this kind of shoreline. The nearest house was about a third of a mile away; half a mile to the north were two powerboats at anchor, and to the west, a mile away across the water, were five empty sand barges and a floating dredge. Otherwise, the whole broad basin of water was ours, and it probably looked not very different from the way it did before white men ever sat foot on Long Island.

It was nearly twilight, and somewhat cloudy, when we dropped anchor, and the air was cooling rapidly. We put on sweaters and jackets, checked our position against shore points to make sure that the anchor was holding firmly, and then relaxed and rejoiced in our solitude, our independence of the shore, and our freedom from telephones, public-address systems, traffic, and organized pleasure. Al and Geoffrey lit the alcohol stove after a while and began cooking. Dinner, which we ate on deck as the light began to fade, consisted of spaghetti *al dente* with meat sauce out of a can, sliced tomatoes with bottled Italian dressing, Bardolino Bolla in plastic coffee cups, and an assortment of cookies, with instant coffee. The air was fresh, the light a fading rosy crepuscule, and never, it seemed to me, did gourmet dine better than this, nor feast seem more Lucullian to sybaritic guest. We sat for a

44

long time in the growing dark; at last I roused myself, boiled water, and washed the dishes, and then lay down on my bunk and fell asleep fully clothed, hearing as though from a great distance the voices of my two shipmates discussing the technique of using the *Tide Tables* and *Tidal Current Tables* in planning tomorrow's trip.

A clap of thunder woke me with a start. Al and Geoffrey were peering up the companionway into blackness, the boat was bobbing and plunging, and the wind was making our rigging sing. With hardly a word to each other, we scrambled above to see whether our anchor line was secure and to study the few lights onshore in order to make certain that our anchor was not dragging. The wind was driving straight across Morris Cove toward us, and the waves it whipped up made *Merrywend* pitch and also swing about from side to side; her wheel even spun over by itself a couple of times in ghostly fashion, responding to pressure on the rudder below. Lightning flared overhead almost continuously—now in bright, jagged streaks, now in broad, pale sheets behind the clouds, and now in quick, darting flickers, like the tongue of a snake—and the thunder crashed and boomed almost without pause. Then, at last, came the rain, lashing across the surface of the water and stinging our faces; we hastily tumbled below, and stood in the cabin looking out as the boat heaved and swung around desperately, saved from destruction only by one twenty-eight-pound anchor dug into the mud on the bottom and fifty feet of good seven-eighths-inch nylon rope. But with these *Merrywend* was as safe as any boat on Long Island Sound, and more comfortable by far than any of the boats tied up in places like the Capri, which must have been bounding and bumping in their confined slips.

The rain stopped after half an hour, and we went out on deck again to watch the storm as it slowly withdrew to the southeast. The air was as fresh and winy as air must have been when only the animals knew Long Island. Chilly, and shivering pleasantly, we stood on deck and sipped a bit of brandy to warm ourselves; when the storm had finally disappeared altogether and the bright stars began to appear toward midnight, we gave in to a sweet fatigue, and went below to collapse into profound and childlike sleep.

WHEN I AWOKE THIS MORNING, it was evident, even from our mooring deep within Morris Cove, that this was a weekday. On the west side of the cove, automobiles were hurrying along a shore road, taking men to the station; the dredge was hard at work over that way, screeching and clanking; and on the Sound itself, visible above the low sandspit to the north of us, no sails were in evidence—only the smokestack of a tug well offshore. From somewhere on the other side of Centre Island, a light seaplane snarled loudly in takeoff, appeared above the trees, and climbed over our heads in the direction of New York City. A few minutes later, another one—a single-engine blue-and-yellow Cessna, with pontoons—banked steeply overhead, tiny and bright against the blue sky above Centre Island, and glided in close to us for a smooth landing a quarter of a mile away. It taxied up to a pier belonging to a large house on the shore, where a man carrying a dispatch case stepped aboard, and in a moment the plane roared off to the west. Later in the day, I learned that the passenger was George F. Baker, Jr., a director of the First National City Bank and the owner of Ventura Air Service, a nonscheduled line that ferries passengers from various points on Long Island to Manhattan. Baker himself is flown directly from his summer home on Morris Cove to the foot of Wall Street, and since his office is at 2 Wall Street, he is able to make the trip in twenty minutes, door to door, as opposed to an hour and a half by car, train, and taxi.

Though the morning was a trifle cool, my companions and I leaped overboard and had a brisk swim before breakfast. We pitied the likes of poor Mr. Baker, who despite mansion and plane, had to go to town to attend to business on this glorious morning. After we'd eaten, we sailed out of Morris Cove and around the perimeter of Oyster Bay Harbor, admiring the fine houses and yachts along the way. Where Oyster Bay Harbor opens into Oyster Bay, the land is quite hilly for Long Island. To our right, on Cove Neck, a sand slope named Cooper's Bluff plunged steeply a hundred and eighty feet down to a bit of beach, and so high above Cove Neck that we couldn't see it from the water was (so our guidebook told us) Sagamore Hill, Theodore Roosevelt's home, which is now a museum. Across the water, on the eastern side of Oyster Bay, was the large, broad peninsula known as Lloyd Neck, rising in some places more than a hundred feet above the shore. From where we were, Lloyd Neck looked practically untouched, but snuggled unobtrusively into its wooded slopes at wide intervals are fine homes and mansions belonging to, among others, Marshall Field, Jr., Stavros Niarchos, some assorted Colgates, Sherman Fairchild, and Ferdinand Eberstadt.

Almost directly below the windows of one of the most sumptuous of these houses was a hideous black-and-white tug-like boat, hard at work oyster-dredging in the waters of the bay. *Frank M. Flower*, she was named, and she was cruising slowly in a tight circle, grinding and rumbling as she went, and dragging something at the end of a heavy cable suspended over her port side from a short boom. When the cable was hauled in, the something proved to be a cylindrical iron-mesh basket, about eight feet long, that had been scraping along the bottom, twenty-five feet below, and gathering up oysters, clams, stones, starfish, shells, and mud. The boom dumped the noisome load into a steel hopper forward, where

47

a powerful stream of water from a fixed hose washed away the mud; everything else then proceeded along a rattling conveyor belt to an area amidships where three mud-spattered fellows stood sorting out the oysters and clams and stuffing them into bags, according to size, and chucking the starfish into a separate heap, which was periodically scooped up and dumped into a killing steam bath.

To oystermen, starfish are not the entrancing creatures they are to children on the beach but the deadly enemies of oysters and clams, around which they wrap their arms and slowly pull the shells apart, in order to feed upon the soft bodies within. For the past decade or so, starfish have been mysteriously on the move, invading the Sound in large numbers and migrating slowly westward to the very edges of the choicest oyster-bed areas—Huntington Bay and Oyster Bay, on Long Island, and the waters off the Norwalk Islands and Branford, in Connecticut—where fifty thousand underwater acres of oyster farms, plus tens of thousands of acres of clam beds, have been cultivated and harvested for generations, and still flourish, despite the heavy modern traffic of sailboats and powerboats only twenty or thirty feet overhead. The oystermen, in despair, are fighting the starfish by dredging them up and destroying them, and also by marking out borders on the sea floor with granules and lumps of certain chemicals that starfish and other oyster predators (most notably a variety of snails called drills, which also raise havoc in oyster beds) are loath to cross. The one thing that the oystermen cannot do is relocate their farms; the Sound has only a limited amount of the kind of protected water and smooth bottom required for oyster culture, and, in any case, it takes years to bring a crop from seed to harvest. Oystermen sow small seedling oysters in quite shallow water on prepared beds of old oyster shells, dredge the seedlings up after a year, and replant them in somewhat deeper water, to spend three more years growing to maturity. Marine biologists in the Bureau of Commercial Fisheries of the Department of the Interior are not at all sure of the reason for the current invasion of starfish, but they speculate that it is probably man disturbing the balance of nature again—this time by congregating in large numbers along the margins of the Sound and polluting its waters with the waste products of modern life. This has killed off either the natural enemies of the starfish or most forms of starfish food, and the starfish either have been freer to multiply or have been spurred into migrating in search of new food. Just how much damage the starfish have caused is a matter of debate, but, between the starfish and a recent sharp decline in the number of oyster fishermen, the total crop is less than a tenth of what it was before the Second World War. And if the starfish don't kill off oystering in Long Island Sound, man may soon do it on his own; the constantly increasing amount of treated and untreated sewage and industrial wastes flowing into its waters is already reaching a critical point in some areas. This past summer, notices from state and county health departments were tacked up on telephone poles on many of the beaches between New York and Stamford forbidding anyone to collect and eat shellfish from the local waters, because of the dangerous pollution. It seems inevitable that the same thing will soon be happening elsewhere along the Sound; every time that a new stretch of superhighway is opened on Long Island, more people buy land, build houses, and utilize the plumbing in them—thus eventually reaching the Sound, and so the oysterbeds. The Great Chain of Being is not always lovely to contemplate. And yet, for the present, one can sail the length of Oyster Bay and into Cold Spring Harbor of a Monday morning in August and feel centuries removed from such dismal developments. All the way in to the head of Cold Spring Harbor, the shores of the bay are wooded and hilly, and only a few houses are visible; aside from anchorages belonging to one small boat club, the water is virtually innocent of moorings and markers, and there is nothing even remotely like the floating hot-dog stand we saw yesterday in Manhasset Bay.

At the inner end of Cold Spring Harbor, where Highway

25A runs along the shore, we could see a restaurant we'd heard of—a place called the Mooring—and since it was nearing noon, we decided to tie up there and lunch in style. Dropping sail, we motored through a narrow passage past a sand bar and into a tiny basin. Here, right at the water's edge, was a long rambling white clapboard building, with a dock running parallel to the shoreline along its front, an awning-covered deck above that, and a few powerboats tied up nearby—a combination that gave it a very salty look. The saltiness was mostly illusion, as we found out when we tried to learn whether there was enough water for our boat at the dockside (it was now dead low tide). Al, a former commander in the Navy, got out the megaphone and hailed the restaurant in his best naval style, crying "Ahoy, Mooring! . . . Ahoy, Mooring!" without getting any reply. "Ahoy, Mooring!" he bellowed again, and we could see a few well-dressed guests on the deck tittering nervously. At last, a waitress with a napkin on her arm came to the railing, and when we asked about the depth, she said, "I don't know what it is, but they all tie up here, so I guess it's all right." I eased *Merrywend* in toward the dock, but about three feet off she went gently but unmistakably aground on mud. We leaped ashore, cursing the waitress softly, tied the boat up as she was, and settled down at a table on the deck for a long lunch while we waited for the tide to rise and float us off. As far as we could tell, we were the only seaborne customers; the rest of the lunchers seemed to be mostly businessmen, local women getting together with their friends, and (we fancied) two or three couples meeting on clandestine business.

(I was not really surprised to find the Mooring's saltiness purely synthetic. In early June I had sailed this way with three other friends late one Saturday afternoon, and seeing the Mooring from out on the water, thought I had found a real mariner's restaurant. We anchored out that time—the dock was already fully occupied by powerboats—washed and dressed, had cocktails, and at 8 P.M. whistled for the launch.

On the way across, we noticed a large parking lot filled with cars behind the restaurant, and thus had our first intimation that all was not so salty. We walked up a gangplank with rope handrails, opened the front door, and stepped into a pure East Side atmosphere: dimlit, smoky cocktail lounge, tinkling piano, close-ordered ranks of well-dressed drinkers at the bar, maître d'hôtel clutching his reservation list, waitresses scurrying about frantically. In our sports clothing, deck shoes, and fresh sunburns, we felt like the certified local color, here to give the refugees from Manhattan the feeling that they were indeed dining at a mariner's restaurant.)

By 1:30 P.M., *Merrywend* was nicely afloat, and we headed her north, to sail out into the Sound, around Lloyd Neck, and into Huntington Bay, on its eastern side. Much of the soil on Lloyd Neck, as on other peninsulas of western Long Island, is pure sand, dozens of feet deep, with a mere film of topsoil. In certain low-lying places, where the sand is naked of any tree cover, floating dredges have been brought in to dig it out and send it off to New York City, in barges, to be sold to builders, and where the dredges have worked long and hard enough, they have sometimes scooped out sheltered little coves, or "gunk holes," as sailors call any tiny haven of the sort, natural or man-made. One of these man-made basins lies off the northwestern tip of Lloyd Neck; the result of years of profitable digging, it is half a mile long and nearly a quarter of a mile wide, and is known as Lloyd Sand Hole to the pleasure-boaters who cram into it on weekends for overnight anchoring. This particular gunk hole has been used by sailors for more than thirty-five years, and in 1956 the traffic became so dense on weekends that Sherman Fairchild, who owned part of the basin shoreline, had summonses served on four boatowners for anchoring on his bottom and walking on his beach. Suffolk County Judge Charles MacLean, Jr., who heard the case, wrote a nineteen-page decision in which, outdoing Solomon, he divided the baby without slaying it: he said that although the basin was man-made, tidal water flowed freely in and out of it, which made it essentially part of the Sound, so boatmen might enter it and sink their anchors in Mr. Fairchild's mud, but they might not come ashore and walk on his beach above the high-water mark. One of the four defendants, who had taken such a walk, was fined twenty dollars for trespassing. From then on, boatowners hewed to the water line, but Mr. Fairchild was apparently not mollified, for he later threw up his hands and gave his part of the shoreline to the Long Island State Park Commission.

This afternoon, not a single visiting boat was to be seen in Lloyd Sand Hole, although fifty or more are often packed in there of a Saturday night. For the next several hours of what was turning into a gray, dull day, we sailed slowly along the broad, irregular end of Lloyd Neck. The air was somewhat hazy, and although Stamford, from which we had started three days ago, was less than eight miles away across the Sound, we could see nothing of it. The haze also hid most of the boats we might have seen, and gave us again the pleasant illusion of being practically alone and wonderfully remote from civilization and its discontents.

The shoreline of Huntington Bay, a wide-mouthed, funnel-shaped body of water, also looked relatively wild and unimproved, but at its southwest corner we passed through a very narrow opening and came abruptly into civilization, in the form of Huntington Harbor. A curving passage a mile and a half long but only a few hundred yards wide, it was dotted with a thousand or more boats lying at moorings, through which a very narrow channel was outlined by a series of nuns and cans—the red cones and black cylinders of the familiar Coast Guard buoys. Despite the large number of craft, the harbor seemed charming to us, because the boats, instead of being regimented into the straight rows characteristic of the Sound's more glittering marinas, were all swinging free around their own moorings, and thus gave the whole place the naïve cluttered look of an old-time port. On either side of the water, moreover, were sloping banks dotted with handsome houses and lawns, and on the west bank a section of Huntington proper that edges down toward the shoreline looked as improbably quaint as the towns that small boys set up around their electric trains. A large green tugboat eased its way through the channel, crew-cut children scooted about in tiny sailing dinghies or outboard motorboats, and, to our left, a flock of swans glided along near the docks of the Huntington Yacht Club. Here we drew up, spoke to the dockmaster, and were assigned an overnight mooring in the middle of the harbor.

Not everyone is charmed by the harbor's cluttered look. Our hosts that evening—Norman and Alice Row, I shall call them, since they prefer not to be identified—are lifetime residents of Huntington, and they expressed deep distress over what has become of their town harbor. Alice, who met us at the Yacht Club dock and took us off to dinner soon after we arrived, began at once to deplore the state of things. "It's heartbreaking," she said as we drove away from the club. "Huntington Harbor used to be so unspoiled and lovely when I was a girl, twenty-five years ago. It was a real picture-book harbor then. And it was still pretty much that way right after the war. Now look at it! It's really shocking—hardly room for another boat in the water. And yet they're about to build a marina at the foot of the harbor and jam in still more. It all really began in 1957, when the town built public launching ramps on Mill Dam Road, here at the inner end of the harbor, and didn't set up restrictions on using them. Anyone at all could come along towing his boat on a trailer, run it down the ramp, and use our harbor as his home port. We've got people here from all sorts of places—even Brooklyn. It's just tragic."

Between the road and the water were some attractive old clapboard houses, and as we passed them she waved a hand toward one of them and continued her threnody. "Friends of mine used to own and love that house, but recently they had to move out. They couldn't stand the racket of the outboard motors all summer long, or having all kinds of people with boats keep dropping in on them and wanting to use their phone and their bathroom. I have relatives who fly to Marblehead every weekend to sail because they simply can't stand conditions around here any longer."

Her relatives may be unusually sensitive, I gathered, for at the Rows' house I learned that the younger generation still finds sailing on the Sound dandy. Indeed, after dinner, Alice reminded Norman, Jr., her thirteen-year-old son, that he had to pack a bag and go to bed early, in order to get up at dawn to leave for Greenwich and three days of class-boat racing. I was surprised at a thirteen-year-old's being involved in organized sailing races, and Norman and Alice explained to me that today there is a growing interest around the Sound in training youngsters for sailboat racing—mostly in thirteen-and-a-half-foot Blue Jays or nineteen-foot Lightnings. To promote this interest, forty-one yacht clubs with junior divisions have formed the Junior Yacht Racing Association of Long Island Sound. Each club runs intramural races all summer, and at the end of the season the best and second-best crews from all the member clubs converge on the club whose boat won the previous year's interclub race. The scores of youngsters who turn up, seabags in hand, are housed and fed in the homes of members of the host yacht club while the races are going on. In addition to these championship races, four regattas are held—far larger affairs, each of them amounting to a kind of nautical junior prom, at which nearly everyone, champion or not, tries to show up. It was to such a regatta, involving over two hundred and fifty boats, that young Norman was going. Over eight hundred teen-agers—all in deadly earnest about sailing—would assemble at the major yacht clubs in Rye, Greenwich, and Stamford, and would either race or watch races for three days. In past summers, I had seen strings of tiny sailboats being towed by powerboats up or down the Sound, looking like families of ducklings hurrying along behind their mother ducks; now I realized that those little boats had been on their way to some host club for class races. All told, there are a couple of thousand junior racing yachtsmen on the Sound, taking part in a couple of thousand intramural and extramural races during the summer; if all of them grow up to be ardent yachtsmen, and teach their children to be ardent junior yachtsmen, the Sound may, in a generation, be as crisscrossed with races on a Sunday afternoon as the Meadow in Central Park is with softball games.

Tuesday, August 13

AT 7 A.M., EXUBERANT SHOUTING WOKE ME, and when I looked across the water toward the yacht club, I saw perhaps twenty teen-agers—including Norman, Jr.—assembling eight Blue Jays and Lightnings into a file to be towed to Greenwich by a large ketch with an auxiliary motor. The morning was gray and windy, and the juniors were in for a choppy and chilly crossing in their little boats, although if it got too rough and uncomfortable they would probably be taken aboard the ketch. In any event, the young people were on their way to Connecticut long before we were ready to start our own day's sail. Emerging around nine from the sheltered harbor into the broader waters of Huntington Bay, we found a brisk south-southeast wind blowing, which heeled *Merrywend* over and gave us advance notice of a fast, wet ride on the open Sound. Our first tack within the bay carried us close to Eatons Neck, the peninsula that forms its eastern boundary. Part way along the shoreline of Eatons Neck is a long sandspit projecting south-southwest and protecting a small cove shaped like an inverted V, which is known as Price

Bend. I had stayed overnight there during a cruise six years ago, and now I felt an impulse to revisit the place, so I altered course and sailed around the southern tip of the sandspit. Price Bend had been a delightful overnight anchorage, I recalled— lonely, unspoiled, and a trifle desolate, with the barren sandspit on one side and, on the other, only a few houses showing through the trees that clothed the slopes of Eatons Neck. However, as we sailed up into Price Bend this morning, I once again heard, like old Marvell, Time's wingëd chariot hurrying near, for now there was, to begin with, a *Capn's Galley* anchored just inside the sandspit, ready, like the one we had seen in Manhasset Bay, to dispense cigarettes, Cokes, and "He-Man's Fried Seafood Plates." The eastern side of the Bend had acquired a number of new houses, and as for the sandspit, a road had been extended out to it and a parking lot and pavilion put up there. These were deserted this morning, but I felt sure that the sandspit would be jammed with cars and bodies on any sunny weekend.

Leaving much improved Price Bend, we returned to Huntington Bay and sailed north along the shore of Eatons Neck toward the Sound, which opened out before us two and a half miles away. Eatons Neck is an interesting bit of territory. A hilly, pear-shaped blob of land, roughly two miles long and a mile wide, it is very nearly an island, being connected to Long Island proper only by a long umbilical cord of sand, along which runs a narrow road. It is thus relatively remote and isolated, even though it is only a few miles by water from Huntington and several other ports. Some three centuries ago, a London merchant named Theophilus Eaton came to America and bought the Neck from the Crown, hoping to found an English settlement there, but at no time until after the Second World War did it attract anything more than a handful of residents; it consisted mostly of large farms, ancient woods, a few fine estates, and a scattering of modest summer homes. Since the war, much of the land has been cut up into lots of from one to three acres. Near the northern end, there is still a sizable patch of untouched woods—kept as a game preserve by its owner, who is Henry S. Morgan, a grandson of J. P. Morgan—and on the northern tip, just beyond Mr. Morgan's woods, and commanding a wide view of the Sound, is a ten-acre tract of open land given over to a lighthouse and to the dock, boat shed, and other buildings of the Eatons Neck Coast Guard Station. The station has a complement of thirty-five men, whose major business is to police the western half of the Sound; the eastern half is policed by a similar station based at a large Coast Guard installation in New London.

The nerve center of the station at Eatons Neck, as I knew from a visit I paid it in the spring, is its radio room, which is set up in a large white frame building a short distance from the shore. There two coastguardsmen monitor the voice channels used most often by ships at sea—notably 2182 kilocycles, the international distress and calling frequency, and 2662 kilocycles, the Coast Guard working frequency. While I was there in the spring, four calls came in on 2182 in the course of one hour: a power cruiser was out of gas, a sailboat had a broken link in the chain drive of its steering gear and was floundering about, and two powerboats wanted to find out if their radio equipment was transmitting loud and clear. The latter two were brusquely told to get off the emergency frequency and use another one; the former two, when it was clear that they were in no immediate danger, were asked to switch over to 2670 (Coast Guard voice common-liaison), and on that channel were asked where they were and in what kind of boat, and were told that help would arrive shortly. (The international distress and calling frequency is kept absolutely clear of everything but life-and-death, or "mayday," calls. Mayday—a corruption, I have been told, of the French *m'aidez!*—is the standard nautical cry for help.) The radio operator then switched his transmitter to 2662 and talked to his own boats on the Sound until he found which two were nearest the distress cases, and dispatched them to lend a hand; the powerboat was given some gasoline, and the sailboat was towed to a nearby port for repairs.

Only a limited number of the pleasure craft on Long Island Sound have radio transmitters aboard (even *Merrywend*, a new, twenty-two-thousand-dollar boat, does not), so during the summer each Coast Guard station keeps several boats cruising around its territory on the lookout for distress cases that might not be able to signal their plight, and usually one boat is detailed to watch over any sizable sailboat race—especially when small sailboats are involved, since these are sometimes knocked over by the dozen on a gusty day. In wild or stormy weather, the patrol boats scout around with particular diligence, looking for powerboats that have ruptured some vital part of their engine system and are wallowing helplessly, and for sailboats whose sails have ripped or that have been dismasted or otherwise disabled. A prolonged, severe storm that has been well advertised in advance is not too much of a problem, since most people have sense enough to stay in harbor on such days, but the summer thunderstorm or line squall, which can blow up in ten or twenty minutes in the middle of a fine day, is a real worry. Chief Warrant Officer George Bannan, the commanding officer of the Eatons Neck Coast Guard Station, told me during my spring visit that in some ways storms on the Sound are worse than storms on the open Atlantic. "When I was in the Navy, I used to think of the Sound as a millpond, but since I've been stationed here in the Coast Guard, I've come to respect it," he said. "It's one of the most treacherous and dangerous bodies of water around. In less than half an hour, it can kick up from a glassy calm to waves six and eight feet high. And what waves! Out at sea, the harder it blows the longer the swells get, so you can ride up and over them without any trouble. But the Sound is shallow—no more than fifty to seventy-five feet deep in most places—and shallow water behaves differently in a blow; you get a short, high chop that's really vicious. It knocks a boat around, makes it tricky to steer and almost impossible to sail, and slops right over you and threatens to swamp you. On a really bad day, we try to use only our new forty-four-foot steel motor-lifeboat, which is hermetically sealed all around, so that no matter how it gets tossed about, it can't be swamped. In fact, it's balanced so that if it's turned upside down, it will right itself. The coxswain, who sits outside, has to be strapped down at the controls with a safety belt, and if the boat turns over, he holds his breath until it rolls back. Takes a good man not to panic at a time like that."

With the aid of this boat—which I have seen boiling along at thirty knots or better—and a number of others, some larger and some smaller, the Coast Guard station at Eatons Neck and the one at New London handle well over a thousand distress calls a year, in addition to helping the innumerable small sailboats that get knocked down. In between times, they handle thousands of non-emergency jobs, such as finding fishermen whose families or employers have urgent messages for them, flagging down, boarding, and inspecting boats, and writing up violations of the law, which may range from wrong-size Coast Guard numbers on the bow to inadequate or outdated fire extinguishers and life preservers. (For serious violations, the Coast Guard can impose fines of up to two hundred dollars.) Besides their lifeboat and inspection work, the Coast Guard boats keep an eye on the navigation lights on bridges, tend and refurbish seven hundred and forty-four buoys and lights around the Sound, check to see that the racing buoys set out by yacht clubs conform to the law, and ferry food and changes of crew out to the offshore lighthouses still manned by coastguardmen. (There are just eight of these left, plus five manned lighthouses on land. Seventy-five other lighthouses, on land and on water, have recently been automated.) More exhilarating but less frequent are such chores as chasing an occasional nautical thief who is making off with a powerboat, retrieving a discontented youngster who has set out for far places in the family cruiser, or searching for a missing husband and finding him anchored in some gunk hole with a companion of whose existence his wife was unaware.

When we had sailed half a mile or so beyond the mouth of Huntington Bay, and could safely clear the tip of Eatons Neck on a starboard tack, we came about and once again headed eastward. The wind, directly on the starboard beam, was strong, and once we had trimmed sail and steadied *Merrywend* on her course, she hit her stride and fairly raced along. Coming to us from the shore, the wind had only a mile or so in which to work on the surface of the angry lead-colored sea, so the waves were not too bad, but on the Connecticut side, ten miles away, things were undoubtedly a great deal rougher. The boat was extremely lively this morning, slicing through the smaller waves and soaring up the slopes of the larger ones, and she heeled over so far that we had to sit with our feet braced firmly against the sides of the cockpit. From time to time, sheets of spray flew out from the bow and across the deck, slapping us smartly in the face. We had put on warm clothes and our hooded foul-weather gear, but the water dripped down our faces, and trickled in around our necks and wrists. Oddly, it was by no means unpleasant; in fact, we rather liked having it dash in our faces and drip off our chins.

Our course took us on a straight line across the long, gentle curve of Smithtown Bay, past Sunken Meadow State Park, San Remo, Nissequogue, and Stony Brook. Except for a tug hauling a couple of barges and two fairly large fishing boats, we saw no one else on the water, and the shoreline—a vaguely defined strip of sand cliffs, beaches, and shallow wooded slopes—seemed, like the sea, to be practically uninhabited. Now and then a few houses or a smokestack or a water tank protruded from the horizon of trees, but except for those, we could indulge in the illusion that we were the first men ever to scud along this perhaps hostile coast, looking for a place to go ashore and explore the hinterland. It struck me as surprising that this sort of illusion was possible only an hour or so out from Huntington Harbor, whose overdevelopment our hostess had lamented so keenly.

Being happily free from any taint of seasickness, by ten-thirty all three of us were ravenously hungry, and we took turns at lurching down into the galley and bringing up handfuls of beer bottles, cold cuts, cheese, and buttered bread. Without slacking off the sails to moderate our speed, we ate intermittently for an hour and a half, making excellent headway all the while. We had passed the lighthouse on Eatons Neck at 10:20 A.M., and at 12:15 P.M. we were abreast of the lighthouse on Old Field Point, having made a perfectly straight alongshore run of nearly fourteen and a half statute miles in just under two hours. This meant that we had travelled at a trifle better than six knots, and for a boat of *Merrywend's* size and type this is just about top speed.

Beyond Old Field Point, the land dropped down to a long sandy beach, which curved away from us. About a mile and a third of the way along this beach, a narrow gap in the sand was marked by two short projecting breakwaters, on which a pair of automatic lights mounted on rather low steel towers flashed at four-second intervals. This was the entrance to Port Jefferson Harbor, where we would spend the night, since the next harbor eastward lay too far away for us to reach it without an unduly long and hard day's sailing. Tacking closely back and forth against the wind in the narrow channel, we worked our way into the harbor, which is a spacious one—a kind of tapering oblong about two miles deep and a mile wide. The wind and waves moderated as soon as we came out of the channel, and we pushed down inside the harbor toward the town dock.

A single glance was enough to reveal that Port Jefferson is torn by conflicting desires—to be a commercial harbor and to be a recreational center. A huge power plant of the Long Island Lighting Company lay on the western side, busily emitting dark smoke from three towering stacks. On the opposite side stood gasoline and oil storage tanks, and at the head of the harbor were cranes of the New York Trap Rock Corporation, noisily unloading sand and rock from barges. Amid all this, a two-decker white ferry named *Catskill* hooted twice, pulled away from her pier, and implacably plowed through the harbor—as she does every five hours—carrying a load of vacationers and tourists across the Sound to Bridgeport. A large fleet of pleasure boats, some of them very handsome and costly-looking, lay at moorings only a quarter of a mile off the New York Trap Rock installation, and right next to it was a sizable marina, with about a hundred and fifty fishing boats and power cruisers tied up at slips.

Dropping sail, we motored up to the town dock—a high wooden structure with a series of old automobile tires hanging along its sides to protect boats from getting banged up on its rough pilings. Here we gassed up, filled our water tanks, took on fifty pounds of ice for our icebox (we had to do all this about every three days), and got permission to lie overnight at one of the moorings of the Port Jefferson Yacht Club. By the time we had motored out to the mooring, it was beginning to rain rather hard. On board a sailboat, one must be emotionally prepared for the necessity of killing time during bad weather, and since all three of us were aware of this, we settled back contentedly to read whatever we could find on *Merrywend's* bookshelf. We alternately read and dozed while the rain pattered on deck and rivulets ran across the portholes. Then, just after 6 P.M., we washed, had a leisurely drink, and cooked dinner, which we ate by the soft light of two kerosene lamps. After dinner, we listened to music and the weather report on the radio, played a few rousing games of Categories, and were in our bunks for the night before 10 P.M.

A BRILLIANT SHAFT OF SUNLIGHT streaming in through a porthole woke me at 6:50 A.M. A cold front had passed through during the night, and the sky was bright blue, the air was nippy, and the wind was coming out of the north-west—exactly the opposite direction from yesterday's blow. I had slept so soundly that I had been unaware of any motion of the boat during the night, but now *Merrywend* was prancing nervously at her mooring, and the wind was moaning in the rigging. I sought a weather forecast on the radio, as I did every morning—and as every careful mariner does—for in a protected harbor or river one can badly underestimate the wind force and the surface conditions outside. Besides, it is important to know the wind direction and the changes in it predicted for the day, so as to plan one's sailing intelligently. (A sailboat can sail diagonally off the wind but not directly into it, so if the wind happens to be blowing head on, it is necessary to tack back and forth, gaining one's objective by working one's way up to it. Only by knowing the wind direction in advance, however, can one study the charts and the current tables and rationally plot a sailing plan to overcome the obstacles of geography and contrary currents.)

From WICC, in Bridgeport, I learned that the wind would be north to northwest, and that was ideal for us, since our course lay to the east and we would therefore not have to tack. But the forecast estimated the wind velocity at twenty-five to thirty-five knots—too much wind for comfort, and very nearly too much for safety—and small-craft warnings had been raised from Block Island to Cape Hatteras. *Merry-wend* was new, stoutly built, and seaworthy, but that wind, coming clear across the Sound from Connecticut, had a twelve- to fifteen-mile fetch to get the surface tumbling—and halfway on our day's journey we would be at the widest part of the Sound, where it would have an even longer fetch. At best, the ride would be wet, uncomfortable, and nerve-racking, and quite possibly it might even be dangerous. A sail fitting or the rigging might give way, and it was even possible that the mast might snap; any of these events would make us dependent on the small thirty-horsepower motor, and between Port Jefferson and the next harbor, at Mattituck, there was a naked, hostile twenty-five-mile stretch of coastline, offering not a single cove, breakwater, or river mouth for shelter.

All through breakfast we debated the matter, and finally we decided to chance it. We went forward on deck and bent on the jib, preparatory to hoisting sail and dropping the mooring. But while we had been having breakfast the wind had risen further, and was blowing straight down the harbor toward us from the Sound. Even within Port Jefferson Harbor, the waves had had whitecaps ever since we got up, and now the whitecaps were beginning to blow off, their foam streaming out ahead of the waves and lacing the dark water. When the wind is strong enough to do this, boats the size of *Merry-wend* are in for a very unpleasant time, and I changed my mind and said we ought to stay where we were until things eased a bit. My friend Al, a bolder sailor than I, argued that there were already a couple of sailboats out. We could see their sails over the sandspits at the harbor mouth, but as we watched them through the binoculars, they both headed back in between the breakwaters, ran down to our end of the harbor, and dropped sail. The smaller of the two was our size, and the other—*Avalon*, out of Greenwich—was fifty-one and a half feet overall, according to our copy of *Lloyd's Register of American Yachts;* we decided that if that big a boat had come back inside after one taste of the Sound this morning, we had better stay at our mooring and make the best of it.

Bundled in sweaters and jackets, we sat in the cockpit reading, or staring at the water and the sky; in harbors all around the Sound, thousands of other summer sailors on their vacation cruises must have been doing the very same thing this morning. The rolling water was deep blue-green, strewn with foam and sun-dazzled toward the east; the azure sky was dotted with scurrying puffs of white cloud; the boats moored all around us were, like *Merrywend*, pitching up and down, their halyards slatting against their masts, and spray breaking out from under their bows. We settled down to a slow rhythm of living suitable to the day—we studied other boats through the binoculars and discussed their lines and rigging, talked desultorily about the technique of handling a boat in a wind like this, visited the galley now and again for snacks, read a little, listened to the radio, and at length, drowsy from sun and wind, collapsed into lethargy. Some time later in the morning we were roused out of it when Geoffrey noticed that a small green-and-white sedan cabin cruiser moored a hundred yards from us seemed to be lying unusually low in the water for a boat her size. For what seemed like an hour, we watched, hypnotized, as she very slowly sank lower and lower. Some piece of plumbing in her galley or her head must have broken under the strain of the ceaseless bouncing around that the boats were being subjected to, and water was slowly filling the cabin and sinking her. Since we had nothing but a cockleshell dinghy, we could not risk rowing over to her, nor could we safely have towed her in with *Merrywend* on a day like this. We blew our compressed-air horn repeatedly to summon help from the yacht club, but the wind tore the sound away, and no one came out. At last, waves began to wash over the coamings into the cockpit, and in another minute or two the pretty little boat sank, stern first, her bright-red cabin cushions floating out through an open window and drifting away over the vexed water. We later discovered that this was not the only casualty of the day, for when we were finally heard and picked up by the club's launch, we saw three other small boats swamped at the docks. Yet, oddly, as soon as we were onshore and in the town proper, the day seemed merely brisk and pleasantly breezy; the remorseless wind and pounding sea were now remote and chimerical. Even when we caught a glimpse of the water as we were walking down Main Street, it seemed sparkling, white-flecked, and lovely, rather than implacable and angry.

With nothing to do but wait for the wind to abate, we spent the rest of the afternoon ambling idly about the town, like sailors on shore leave. Port Jefferson, unfortunately, does not have much to delight the casual visitor. Its Main Street, running straight back from the waterfront, is reminiscent of the main street of many a moribund New England town; the sidewalks are cracked and broken, the buildings dingy, and the standard features uninteresting—a faded hotel, a liquor store, a real-estate office with bleached photographs posted in its window of houses for sale, a drugstore, a laundromat, a supermarket, a used-car lot, a Presbyterian church, a Methodist church, a Masonic Temple, and a movie house. A spotted frog hopped across the sidewalk in front of us, and a brown dog slept in the street near one of the parking meters. We did see some handsome Colonial houses scattered around town, but most of them needed paint and had a generally seedy look.

It was not always thus. In the nineteenth century, Port Jeff, as it is known to its residents, enjoyed a Golden Age. Though the village was founded in 1655, it had little importance until the era of the big sail-driven whaling vessels and coastwise cargo schooners. Then, thanks to its large, deep-water harbor, it became a shipbuilding center and a major home port for sailing captains, who kept their boats in its harbor during the winter and built fine wooden houses nearby. The twentieth century brought the switch to steam-driven vessels, and shipbuilding moved away to larger facilities, on the mainland; during the First World War there was one more burst of shipbuilding at Port Jeff, but after that the town sank back into somnolence, and its population has remained virtually unchanged ever since, at about three thousand persons. Because it is the only major harbor on the eastern half of Long Island that is on the Sound proper, it is the home base of a ferry service to Connecticut; the power plant and the rock-and-sand installation, both of which rely on barges to bring in their voluminous supplies of raw materials, are there for the same reason. But little happens in Port Jeff itself, and most of its inhabitants work in plants scattered around Long Island—among them Grumman Aircraft, Republic Aviation, R.C.A., and the Brookhaven National Laboratory. Port Jeff, which only recently became an incorporated village, is growing aware of the conflicting aims of industry and the summer crowd, but there seems to be a nearly even division of opinion among its people over whether it ought to try to develop its port industrially or turn it into a prime recreational attraction. To judge by a copy of the Port Jefferson *Times* that I bought and read over a malted milk in the drugstore, Mayor Robert L. Robertson was flatly for positive fence-straddling; he was in favor of doing both simultaneously, without regard to their incompatibility.

While Al and Geoffrey went off to do a little shopping, I studied the front page to see what the top news stories were in Port Jeff this week. One was a feud that the village was having with Suffolk County—the village wanting to set up its own police force, and the county, which had been policing Port Jeff for many years, fighting the move. Another quoted Malcolm X as stating that Black Muslim meetings were already being held in Suffolk County, but denying a rumor that a Black Muslim mosque was being built in Wyandanch. A third story revealed that the Calvary Baptist Church would shortly begin its two-week Vacation Bible School with a course on the theme "Living with Christ." A photograph showed Harry Merchant, a fuel dealer, putting a clam into the mouth of Robert Merkle, another fuel dealer, at the annual outing of the Oil Heat Institute of Long Island.

Having exhausted the Port Jefferson *Times*, I returned to the news counter and picked up a copy of the *Long Island Traveler–Mattituck Watchman*, which had caught my eye because Mattituck would be our next stop. The big story was that eighteen-year-old Ruth Ann Brennan of Bridgehampton had been crowned 1963 Potato Queen at the Potato Blossom Ball in Riverhead. Other exciting items told of a picnic scheduled by the Republican Club, a talk delivered to the Rotarians by a veterinarian, and the dedication of a restored old house in Orient by the Oysterponds Historical Society.

Of greater interest to me was a report of two boating accidents in nearby waters and the paper's comment on them. A speeding powerboat towing a water skier had rammed into a small fishing boat, sinking it instantly and injuring both its occupants, and an outboard motorboat being run wide open by a teen-age boy had hit and sunk a small sailboat, seriously injuring its skipper, who was teaching a young girl to sail. On an inside page, the *Traveler* ran an angry editorial titled "Danger on the Water," in which it called for better supervision and control of boating, with particular emphasis on the thrill-seekers in fast outboards. I felt this was by no means an unfair comment, for a Coast Guard publication that Chief Bannan had given me when I talked to him reported that over two thirds of all fatal boating accidents involved outboard motorboats. Pleasure-boating has grown so fast that little social control has been imposed on it, though the need is already plain. No license is necessary to operate an outboard motorboat, and in most states just about anyone may launch himself upon the water and zip away at twenty or twenty-five knots without first having to prove any boat-handling skill or any knowledge of the rules of nautical right-of-way, safety procedures, or ordinary boating etiquette. (Most harbor police, when they put up signs limiting speed, use the term "m.p.h.," because so many outboard enthusiasts have no idea what "knots" are.) I myself, in the course of a brief get-acquainted cruise in *Merrywend* earlier in the season, had almost been stove in by a lady in a flowered green dress driving a fast plastic runabout, who cut in front of me in a narrow channel as though we were in mid-Manhattan traffic. She must have supposed I had brakes and could stop, or, at best, she was completely ignorant of the fact that sailboats, with tons of lead in their keels for stability, have considerable momentum and, even when sails are slacked or the engine is thrown into reverse, keep going for quite a while. I managed to miss her by inches, but she glowered at me, clearly regarding me as an incompetent skipper.

Al and his son returned to the drugstore shortly before 6 P.M., and we proceeded to the Whalers' Inn, a restaurant on Main Street that was decorated to resemble the interior of an old whaling ship, and where Al and I solaced ourselves for our lost day of sailing with numerous whiskey sours before dinner. After eating, we walked back to the yacht club and looked for the boy in charge of the launch, but he had already gone home. Over at a nearby gasoline dock, happily, we found a teen-ager in foul-weather gear who, for a dollar, ferried us out through the rough water in a clumsy wooden rowboat with a small outboard motor, and deposited us, half soaked, on *Merrywend*. Our boat was warm and dry within, and after we had changed our clothes, we went up to the cockpit and watched the sun set in a superbly clear sky beyond the harbor mouth. All three of us then wilted suddenly from the long hours of wind and pitching about. Meaning to read for a little while, I lay down on my bunk, fully clothed, and fell asleep at 9:30 P.M. without having washed, undressed, or made up my bunk. Except for momentary discomforts caused by objects in my pants pockets, when from time to time I rolled over, I spent a perfectly fine night in this fashion—something I feel certain I could not do on land under any conditions. But that is yet another reason men love getting away onto the sea; something elemental and natural in them comes to the surface,

displacing the overly civilized, and they recognize in it an old
self, long forgotten and long forbidden, but dear and welcome.

ANOTHER BRILLIANT, MINT-FRESH, CHILLY MORN-
ING, with the same northwest wind sweeping the length of
Port Jefferson Harbor, but this time the radio forecast wind
velocities of only ten to twenty knots. Though waves slapped
at the boat and rocked it about, there was no savagery in them,
and their whitecaps were not flying ahead of them but spilling
smoothly down their slopes. As soon as we had finished breakfast, we hoisted sail, slipped our mooring, and tacked out to
the Sound, where, having put ourselves about a mile offshore, we took up an easterly heading for Mattituck. We had
chosen to bend on the genoa jib—a somewhat larger foresail
than the working jib—to make the most of our favoring wind,
and now we bowled along. Because we were going more or
less with the wind, we did not pound into the waves it was
creating but rode them, rising and falling in a measured, majestic fashion. The sunlight on our white sails dazzled us, the
sea about us was a rich blue, and the only sounds we heard
were the strident cries of sea gulls overhead, the faint hiss of
the water foaming past us, and the rushing sounds behind us
where our dinghy danced and frisked along at the end of its
painter. There behind us, the entire Sound seemed clean and
fallow; directly ahead of us the open water was as empty as if
there were no land for thousands of miles; to our right,
stretching out far into the distance forward, was the long, low

line of the North Fork of Long Island; and to our left, ten or fifteen miles across the water, lay the Connecticut coast, a dim line sloping away from us toward the northeast and disappearing below the horizon. Bridgeport and New Haven were over there, but they looked faint and faded, their gas tanks and smokestacks and dingy air barely visible through the glasses. If we chose not to look at them, we could imagine that all the world's air and water were still pure and clean.

The Long Island shoreline here and for the next forty miles —much farther than we would sail today—is quite unlike that of Connecticut and New York, or, for that matter, of Long Island itself back around Port Washington, Oyster Bay, and Huntington. Here the coast is virtually straight as far as the eye can see—entirely without promontories, inlets, bays, or islands. It consists of a line of sand cliffs—usually rising from a narrow beach—that range from ten or twenty feet in height up to as much as a hundred feet and are topped by a green icing of shrubbery or scrub pine. It looks like a great cake of sand that has been sliced by some gargantuan knife. The cliffs were formed by the fourth, and last, glacier of the Pleistocene Ice Age, which shoved an unthinkably huge mass of sand and broken rock across the valley that is now the bottom of the Sound, and jammed it up against an accumulation of rock, gravel, and earth deposited on an underlying ridge by the previous glaciers. When, after tens of thousands of years, the last glacier melted away, it left behind a steep, clean-cut "contact slope," or impression of itself; this mold of the glacier's frontal edge, somewhat eroded by the winds and waters of the past twenty-five thousand years, was what we were looking at all morning. From our charts, we could see yet another sign that the ice had pushed this far and no farther; the markings showed rocks strewn through the water just off the beach all along here. The ones that protruded from the water, and also some that did not, had names such as Low Tide Rock, Two Pigs and Old Sow, and Fishing Rock, but scores of others were nameless, appearing on the chart only as asterisks. They

71

had all been torn loose from the surface of New England, shoved hundreds of miles across hills and valleys, and dropped here by the ice as it melted, to provide, twenty-five thousand years later, a nasty lot of work for the makers of nautical charts.

On top of the sand cliffs, scattered houses peeped through the trees, and on the beach occasional cabins, and even one sizable beach house, were to be seen, but none of these touches of civilization could change the sailor's view of the coast as an entirely unfriendly one. In a storm, it would offer no least possibility of shelter; one would have to go back to Port Jefferson or far ahead to Mattituck, or clear across the widest part of the Sound to Connecticut. Moreover, the hidden rocks made it dangerous to hug the coast during a storm in an effort to keep track of one's position. If a boat should be disabled or get lost owing to poor visibility, it could easily blunder onto the hidden rocks and be broken to bits in a few minutes. Even on a fine day like this, a mariner looking at his chart of the coast could hardly avoid such thoughts.

At about 11 A.M., a small white sloop appeared astern of us and gradually overtook us. To any sailboat man, the spectacle of a smaller boat outsailing him is both a challenge and a threat. We checked the wind direction and, finding that it was now almost dead astern, decided to try running wing and wing—the genoa far out on one side and the mainsail on the other. Though this maneuver makes for tricky steering, it did increase our speed a trifle. Nevertheless, the little sloop, sailed singlehanded by a youngish man wearing a most unnautical wide-brimmed straw hat and checked blue shirt, slowly overhauled us and then passed us a few hundred yards to starboard. We looked on, glum and annoyed, until he had pulled a little ahead, when Al let out a derisive hoot. "Exhaust smoke!" he shouted. "He's using his motor! No wonder he's beating us. And he doesn't even know enough to put out his flag." Sailing etiquette calls for a yacht's ensign to be displayed at her stern whenever power is being used, and while it is bad enough to use power and sail simultaneously—it's rather like wearing a belt and suspenders—one has to do it now and then, but to appear to be only sailing when one is also using power is very bad form. We felt restored in our self-esteem and thoroughly contemptuous of the skipper of the little sloop.

Stripped to our shorts and basking in the sunshine of what had become quite a warm day, we completed an uneventful trip to the mouth of Mattituck Inlet, and at a little after 2 P.M., five hours from the time we had cleared Port Jefferson, we sailed in between two more rock breakwaters jutting out from the otherwise nearly featureless coastline. From out on the Sound, only these breakwaters were visible; there wasn't a sign of a town or a harbor, and no wonder, for the chart showed us that they lay two miles inland. Inside the break-waters, the wind failed, and we proceeded on the motor into a narrow canal—actually a dredged-out stream—running through a salt-grass marsh. This took us past *John A. Lodini* and *Charles F. McElroy*—two barges of the New York Trap Rock Corporation—and then past a gasoline dock, some fishing boats tied up at a small marina, and a couple of drab-looking canalside restaurants. After that, it meandered through low-lying pine-covered land, where occasional modest summer homes appeared, with rowboats drawn up on the muddy banks. Finally, we rounded a gentle curve and entered an irregularly shaped basin about a third of a mile long. A score of boats, both sail and power, were anchored in the middle of it, and half a dozen others were tied up at two small docks at the far end, where a road from the village came directly to the water's edge. The atmosphere in this harbor, we could see at once, was homey and unsophisticated. On board several of the anchored boats, men and women in simple sailing clothes were puttering around at various chores, and children were playing. One roomy powerboat had a collapsible playpen set up on its foredeck, in which a baby was busy with toys that had sensibly been tied down. A couple of ten-year-olds were sailing around among the anchored boats in a dinghy, which they had probably rigged up the moment their parents dropped anchor. In most of the quiet harbors and anchorages around the Sound, big sailboats whelp little ones in this fashion in the late afternoon.

At one of the two small docks, we rented space to tie up overnight for a fee of $3.30, payable to the town harbor master. Onshore, a few yards away, was a neat white cinder-block building in which, the harbor master informed us, there were showers and washbasins available for the use of visitors. Since we had been cruising for seven days without a chance to stand under hot running water, we hurried ashore and indulged in the intense joys of shaving, showering, and dressing in clean clothes. Deprivation, I think, is the key to keener pleasure; your true voluptuary is not the continuously self-indulgent man, but the one who denies himself for a while and then truly revels in his enjoyments. Feeling virtually reborn and totally at peace, we sat in our cockpit sipping long, cold drinks and studying the scene around us. Mattituck is one of a number of simple port villages on Long Island Sound that have preserved much of their old identity, and offer the visitor shelter, supplies, quiet streets with a few plain stores, and some fine old houses but no antique shops, art movies, Saturday-night dances, or night clubs with New York talent. The yachtsmen who frequent such places are generally more sports-minded than status-minded; for them boating is not a form of countryclubbing but a form of camping. As we looked around us, surreptitiously using the binoculars now and then, we saw many a placid domestic scene. On a small cabin cruiser named *Jay Aye*, which was tied up near us, a middle-aged couple were taking their ease, the husband reading a book and the wife writing a letter; on a Chris-Craft a youngish man was touching up the varnish around a window while his wife and twelve-year-old daughter brought dishes and silver out of the galley and arranged them on a table in the cockpit; out in the middle of the harbor children swam or

74

rowed or sailed while their parents sat resting on board their boats. A small black tugboat, squat and grimy, chugged up to our dock and tied up, and two husky men in plaid shirts and baggy pants got off and headed for the showers while their wives, a couple of square-cut Tugboat Annies, hauled out an assortment of wet blankets and sheets (the tug evidently leaked when spray came over her deck) and festooned the superstructure with them. Near them, paying no attention to anyone or anything, a stubble-faced middle-aged man sat, with his dog, in a small open powerboat that had a single bunk stuffed under the forepeak; like an old bachelor's quarters in a rooming house, his cockpit had cracked linoleum on the floor, a scratchy portable radio, and, strewn all about, pipes, tobacco, charts, pencils, fishing gear, and rusty beer-can openers.

On the opposite side of our dock lay an interesting-looking medium-sized white powerboat named *Très Gaie*, with a long foredeck made of narrow planking that curved off on either side; it reminded me of the hood of a '32 Duesenberg. In the roofed-over cockpit, a young couple and a middle-aged one were having drinks, and I left *Merrywend*, crossed the dock, and struck up a conversation with the older man, who was small, worn-looking, and affable. He told me that his name was Irving Eales, and that he was a painting contractor from Huntington, but that he shunned crowded Huntington Harbor and kept his boat just outside Price Bend, near a little house that his son-in-law—the younger man on board—owned on Eatons Neck. *Très Gaie*, he said, was a 1931 Elco—I had not been far off in time in seeing the likeness to the Duesenberg—and thirty-one feet over all. She had a single engine of a hundred and fifteen horsepower—not very much by contemporary standards. "She was designed to do only about eight knots maximum, and even if I have to put in a new engine someday, I won't put more power in her," Eales said. "It wouldn't be good for her. Anyway, I don't understand the desire for speed out on the water. If you're in a hurry to get someplace, go by car or plane. When I'm in a boat, I want to cruise around at six knots or so and enjoy the view, not drive at twenty-five knots without the time to relax and look at things." Eales's weekend boating habits were simple and family-oriented. "The four of us—my wife, daughter, son-in-law, and myself—usually go out Friday evening and cruise around the local waters," he said. "Then we drop the hook in some little harbor, if we can, or tie up at a dock in a quiet place like this. If the water's clean, we go swimming, and then we cook dinner on board. We stay away from big marinas and fancy restaurants. Sometimes, though, we'll go ashore and see a movie or go bowling. But if there's a good moon, we like to hoist anchor after dinner, run around in the moonlight awhile, and then come back and anchor for the night. It's a fine way to live."

Saying goodbye to Eales, I strolled on down the dock to chat with the harbor master, who was talking to several boatmen at the end of the pier. A tall, lean-featured man in his early fifties named Tom Reeve, he had a hint of New England twang in his speech, and I asked where he was from. He'd never even been to New England, it turned out, and I remembered that historically and culturally the eastern end of Long Island has always been tied more closely to New England than to New York City. "Been here all my life," Reeve said. "I was born and still live in a house within sight of this harbor. My father used to take out fishing parties from this very place, and on a stormy night he'd go all the way to the channel mouth to hang out a kerosene lamp where the electric flasher is now."

The facilities in Mattituck Harbor looked quite new to me, and I asked about them.

"We always had the creek and this basin, and many years ago, when I was a boy, I used to see three-masted schooners come in here during a bad blow," Reeve said. "But the harbor was just a makeshift. Finally, about seven years ago, the county dredged the channel and the basin, and built the docks and the comfort station, and next year the federal government,

76

which has decided to designate Mattituck a 'port of refuge,' will redredge it and improve it further. We've been getting pretty busy here the last five, six years. On a nice summer weekend, I'll count fifty or sixty boats in the basin and a dozen more at the docks. Mattituck appeals mostly to the quiet sort —there aren't any gin mills around here—and some people like it so much that they come from far away and stay right here at my dock for a week at a time."

Just as I was wondering what benefit Mattituck could get out of all this apart from the small docking fees, I noticed a sign near the bathhouse that answered my question; it proclaimed that the shopping center lay straight ahead. Two blocks up Love Lane, past a dozen quiet old houses, are the Long Island Rail Road station and a shopping center of perhaps fifteen stores. A few blocks beyond are the church and the main residential area, leafy, quiet, and Colonial. The livelier aspects of Mattituck life—consisting of such diversions as a dance hall, packed with teen-agers on weekends, and a tenlane bowling alley with a bar and a television set—are exiled to a highway outside town. After dinner on board *Merrywend*, Al, Geoffrey, and I took a walk to look all this over briefly. When we returned, Al went below to write a letter to his wife, and Geoffrey and I sat on deck admiring the stars and listening to the subdued, friendly sounds of life on nearby boats. I asked Geoffrey how he liked the trip thus far. He had learned small-boat sailing when he was a very young boy, but this was his first cruising experience, and I was curious about what it meant to him, and also whether a seventeen-year-old could unbend enough to tell me.

"It's just the most fantastic experience of my whole life!" he burst out. "It's so completely different! The boat seems like a world in itself. We have everything we need on board, we decide what we want to do, and we work together to accomplish each day's trip. We take care of ourselves and are self-sufficient. Everything is unified. There's a sense of—well, of completeness about it." He flapped his hands helplessly. "I don't know," he said. "There just aren't any words for it."

I said I thought he had found some very good ones.

After a few minutes of companionable silence, we got up and adjusted our dock-lines to allow for the change of tide during the night. Then we went below, had some cookies and milk, and turned in.

Friday, August 16

THIS MORNING DAWNED bright and sunny but rather chilly for mid-August. Morning sounds rose all about us: children's shouts and laughter, the piercing note of a whistling teakettle in someone's galley, the clank of a chain as someone else hoisted anchor in the harbor, the deep cough and roar of a powerful motor being started up, the voices of men greeting each other and comparing notes on the day's weather forecast. Voice on the dock: "A fellow who just came in from fishing says the waves are running three foot high out there this morning." Second voice, dejectedly: "No kidding! Well, I'm staying here for the day if that's the case." For our part, we relied on the official weather report, which told us that the wind would be much the same as it was yesterday— ten or fifteen knots, from the northwest—so we weren't uneasy about putting out; even if the waves were three feet high, they wouldn't make us pound and work hard, for we and the waves would be going the same direction. We motored down the creek, passed beyond the breakwaters at 9:35 A.M., and took up a course northeast-by-east, which would carry us parallel to the shore along the remaining twenty miles of the

78

North Fork. Very soon, we settled down, as we had yesterday, to a long, lazy, regular movement, the bow slowly rising and falling, the foam curling away, the wheel steady and easy to handle, and it occurred to me that this was what it must have been like in earlier centuries for merchantmen sailing in the kindly and reliable trade winds. Once again the horizon astern of us and to our left consisted of nothing but water, though during the day, as we proceeded from the widest part of the Sound into its narrowing eastern end, Connecticut slowly reappeared. To our right and stretching far ahead of us was the familiar strip of tree-topped and rock-strewn sand cliffs and beaches, but it was not quite as straight or as high as it had been yesterday, and it grew slowly flatter and scrubbier as the day passed, until it dwindled a couple of times to little more than a sandspit between the Sound and the waters of the bays on the other side. A muffin-shaped lump of green slowly rose out of the Sound straight in front of us—Plum Island, a mile beyond Orient Point, which is the tip of the North Fork. Through the strait between them, known as Plum Gut, ocean water rushes into the Sound, and Sound water rushes back into the ocean, at a speed of as much as four knots. Plum Gut is only one of several apertures where this happens, though; across the twenty-three miles between Orient Point and Watch Hill—the very end of the Sound—stretches a string of islands and shoals, and through all the passages of deep water between them the tidal current flows. Our plan was to sail through Plum Gut today and double back inside the North Fork about nine or ten miles to Greenport, which, though it isn't on the Sound proper, is the major North Fork harbor for Sound mariners, and to return to Plum Gut tomorrow and proceed northeast along the islands and across The Race toward Watch Hill.

Orient Point is a barren, wind-scoured sandspit occupied by a rock-strewn beach, an old white clapboard hotel, and a scattering of houses and telephone poles. Sometimes, where a great point of land reaches out to meet the sea, the effect is majestic or dramatic; so it is with the capes and promontories of Maine and California, and with Land's End, in Cornwall. Orient Point is different. Even on this sunny summer day, it looked merely impoverished and pathetic—a place where the land had not so much boldly stopped as just given up. We had no time, however, to try to extract any meaning from this fact, for Plum Gut, with its powerful currents and its tide rips, takes careful boat-handling, especially when one is trusting to sail rather than to power. Besides, there is heavy traffic here, Plum Gut being the most convenient route for fishing boats and cruisers on their way between the Sound and Montauk or Block Island. During our brief passage through Plum Gut, we saw three sailboats (they were all using their motors to buck the current), a dozen powerboats, a Coast Guard buoy tender, and a huge gray ferry on its way from Orient Point to New London, twenty miles to the north-northeast.

Having rounded Orient Point, we headed back southwest, through Gardiners Bay, paralleling the shore of the North Fork. To our left lay Gardiners Island, hazy and vague in the distance, and far beyond it, half-imagined, the long line of the South Fork, ending in Montauk Point. Dead ahead were the green hills of Shelter Island, an anomalous piece of Westchester countryside dropped into the water between the two forks of eastern Long Island; Greenport, our destination, lay beyond it, on the North Fork itself. In midafternoon, after a day of seeing very few other craft, except in Plum Gut, one fishing boat after another began passing us, heading into Greenport: squat, frumpy oyster boats; tuglike commercial fishing boats with cranes to handle their nets; drab, stained charter boats; and private fishing boats with tall aluminum poles, for tuna fishing, swaying, willowy, and live, as the sleek hulls pitched through each other's wakes.

Greenport came into view when we rounded Hay Beach Point, on Shelter Island. Most of the town waterfront is straight, yet since it lies inside the North Fork, with Shelter Island facing it only three quarters of a mile away, a stone breakwater at the northeast end suffices to make it a thoroughly sheltered harbor. Unlike most of the places we've visited, Greenport had the look of a real working port. At the eastern end of the waterfront were old, unpainted piers and pilings, gray and splintery. The carcasses of two once-proud schooners from the days of the coastal trade lay on their sides nearby, half submerged and rotting, the slimy brown remains of their decks almost vertical. White New England-style houses, some with widows' walks surmounting them, sat snugly on neat grass lawns above a sea wall, and beside them was a busy shipyard with a large, hangarlike work shed, from which we heard the clanging and buzzing of hammers and power saws as shipwrights worked on everything from Lightnings to tugboats. Beyond all this, in the main area of active waterfront, where a number of docks jutted out into the water side by side, hundreds of boats of every description were tied up in a superb jumble, while on the shore we could see an even more disorderly conglomeration of gas pumps, bait shacks, marine-supply stores, restaurants, and parking areas, along with the backs of the various shops facing on Greenport's Main Street. Unlike a modern marina, this waterfront has grown up over many generations, and this, I suppose, is the reason for its pleasant air of confusion and its feeling of authenticity.

We tied up at a large gasoline dock at one end of the waterfront area, where I knew we could stay for several hours, since we were going to have dinner at Claudio's Restaurant, at the foot of the dock. After boiling some water and shaving and dressing, Al and Geoffrey and I ambled into Claudio's. Quite unlike the Mooring, at Cold Spring Harbor, this is a genuinely nautical restaurant; apart from the fact that the interior is tricked out with splices, marlinespikes, cleats, blocks, and other pieces of boating gear, a number of its patrons that evening, as usual, were dressed in boating clothes and looked burned or bleached and cheerfully weary. (I was told, though, that on Saturday nights a rather dressed-up crowd of nearby summer residents comes along fairly late, after the mariners have stumbled off to their bunks.) On the menu, a large sheet of green cardboard, a piece of dreadful doggerel celebrated the highlights of Greenport's long history. While wincing at the spavined meter and threadbare rhymes, I gathered that since the middle of the eighteenth century the town has been the home port of a large variety of boats, including square-rigged merchantmen, coastwise schooners, clipper ships, whalers, oyster boats, commercial fishing boats, and even the America's Cup defender of the 1930 season, *Enterprise*.

Greenport is no longer much of a cargo port, functioning today principally as a haven for private cruising boats and for fishing boats, both private and charter. Fishermen starting out from Greenport are in an excellent strategic position, since from here it is just a short run to the deep-sea-fishing areas of Block Island Sound, beyond Orient Point, and only a bit farther to Montauk and the open Atlantic, where commercial fishermen can find schools of menhaden, and people fishing for sport can find tuna and striped bass. For amateur fishermen with less ambitious aims, it is an even shorter run past Plum Island to The Race, through which large schools of fish like porgy and flounder enter the Sound. To some extent, it is the rush of the tide that carries these swarms into the Sound, but to a larger extent it is subtle tropisms and sense perceptions, drawing them in through The Race and clear down the length of the Sound in search of the microorganisms or small fish on which they feed. The interplay of many forces, including weather, tides, and variations in the abundance of prey, makes for large fluctuations in the yearly catch. Within the Sound, for instance, commercial fishermen took 815,500 pounds of porgy in 1959 but only 179,500 in 1960. The flounder take likewise runs heavy some years and light in others, and, for that matter, may be good one month and practically nonexistent a month or two later; in 1959, according to data from the United States Fish and Wildlife

Service, commercial fishermen caught 105,000 pounds of flounder in the Sound in May and 65,000 pounds in June, but in July, which is ordinarily a good flounder month, they were able to take a mere 5,000 pounds, for reasons that no one seemed to know. Other species that are caught in sizable, if irregular, quantities in the Sound include butterfish, sea bass, sturgeon, weakfish, and white perch, and once in a while, unpredictably and briefly, bluefish and mackerel will swarm into the Sound in great numbers. Most of these edible fish are migratory, and do not live in the Sound all year but come into it seasonally in search of the minnows and other tiny fish that do make the Sound their permanent home. Sharks, too, come in, also probably in pursuit of small fish, but the larger sharks remain at the eastern end of the Sound. Near Orient Point and Plum Island, dogfish sharks up to five feet, dusky sharks up to nine feet, and sand sharks up to twelve feet are always present in the summertime, and half a dozen other large species turn up on occasion. Some of the smaller sharks push on westward; sand sharks a foot or two long are common throughout the Sound, and a four- or five-footer of one species or another has now and then been seen blundering along as far west as Greenwich, or even City Island. It is less well known that both porpoises and seals fairly often penetrate the Sound. Since the seals do so in winter, not many people see them, and reports that they have been seen are generally scoffed at; in the spring of 1963, though, a couple of seals were photographed sunning themselves on rocks in Captain Harbor, off Greenwich, and the picture appeared in a local paper, confounding the doubters.

Numerically speaking, the principal inhabitants of the Sound, as of so many parts of the ocean, are plankton—the usually microscopic protozoa, diatoms, and other tiny animals and plants that drift on or near the surface. The Sound happens to be an excellent breeding ground for many of these forms of life. It is sheltered, it is rich in nutrient wastes, and, most important of all, it is shallow enough for at least a trace of sunlight to penetrate to the bottom nearly everywhere. This is essential to the growth of the vegetable micro-organisms, or phytoplankton, which use energy derived from the sunlight to metabolize mineral salts in their environment into their own living substance, just as plants on land do; in fact, biologists refer to the rapid multiplication of plankton under good conditions as "blooming." Phytoplankton constitute the first link in the feeding chain on which all life in the sea depends; they convert chemicals and sunlight into vegetable tissue, and the animal micro-organisms, or zooplankton, "graze" on them and convert their substance into animal proteins, which become food for small fish, which, in turn, become food for larger fish and for men. People who use the Sound, whether for pleasure or for profit, are usually unaware of the existence of these trillions of micro-organisms floating in the water. Every once in a while, though, a combination of just the right temperature, sunlight, and nutrient material in the water will produce a bloom of such proportions that in some places the water of the Sound will become turbid, or else will be covered with an oily brown film. A more aesthetic manifestation of the proliferating plankton is the appearance, rather rarely, of nighttime bioluminescence—a ghostly greenish-gold flickering in the water, in coves and in streams emptying into the Sound in which there happens to be a large representation of species that are capable of producing a cold light, similar to the light of fireflies. Why plankton should have developed this trait is a mystery to marine biologists. Anyone taking a nocturnal swim in a bay where these types are present in sufficient density will have the ethereal and godlike experience of creating light with every movement of his body. The plankton glow briefly when disturbed, and any stirring of the water with the hands or feet creates clouds of greenish-white light—tiny nebulae of glowing motes, too small to be seen individually, though if one scoops up the water, or splashes it against one's chest, a thousand pinpoints of light sparkle on the skin for an instant as the drops run down. In certain harbors of the Sound, over the years, I have also seen the oars with which I was rowing set up bright whorls in the black water, and sometimes even an anchor line, when the current is flowing past it in the night, will trail a flickering, luminous wake.

After dinner at Claudio's, we took a walk around the Greenport docks, to look at the boats. Hundreds of sight-seers who had come by auto were doing the same thing, making a kind of evening *passeggiata* on the waterfront. With their children in tow, the sight-seers passed by the small, dowdy tugs and the dozen or so frowzy charter boats, and hurried on to those parts of the docks where the larger and more lavish private yachts were to be seen. They stared in wonder at such as *Paumanock II* of Amityville, a fifty-one-foot Dutch-built powerboat, and *Franruss,* a sixty-foot Chris-Craft of East Rockaway. Neither boat's owner seemed to be aboard at the time, but each had left the curtains drawn back on the windows of his saloon, and the lamps lit, with the result that the shuffling, land-bound public, as well as owners of more modest boats, could peer through the windows and vicariously enjoy the way of life of the well-to-do. Other boats, both power and sail—there were a few of the latter —had people aboard, sometimes in the saloons and cabins, but more often sitting on deck, where they smoked and talked, carefully ignoring (though possibly enjoying) the envious stares of the passers-by.

Those who prefer sail are usually contemptuous of power-boats and refer to them as "stinkpots," and to their owners as "stinkpotters." My own preference is for sail, but I had tried—with only partial success—to understand the motiva-tions and joys of the powerboaters, and I now decided to make one final attempt in this direction. A dark-haired, some-what balding man in his forties was sitting on the afterdeck of a handsome, medium-sized power cruiser, and I introduced myself to him. Joe Poletti (as I will call him) told me he was a dental technician in New Haven. "This here's an 'Egg Harbor' sedan cruiser," he said. "She's thirty-seven feet long and draws three and a half. That's deep for a boat this size, but it makes her fabulously seaworthy. And she's so well put together and fitted out so nice that she's a real home on the water for us. Come below and I'll show you." We went down several steps into the main cabin, where his wife, Gina, was busy making dinner at the stove, and a large ungainly adolescent boy was sprawled on a tufted sofa reading a magazine. "Look at this," said Poletti earnestly, "—a three-place burner. Propane. None of the mess and bother of alcohol. An exhaust fan! Formica-topped worktable! Look at the sink—hot and cold running water! No hand-pumping, no boiling up water all the time. Everything's done electrically, pulling power off the dock. When we shove off, the engine heats the hot water and the generators keep the batteries up. Look behind Gina there—not just a refrigerator, but a freezer!" He opened a door behind his wife and smiled fondly upon the shelves packed with frozen foods. "Speaking of hot water," he said, slamming the door shut, "how do you like this?" He opened a door on the other side of the cabin and showed me a bathroom, done up in white-and-gold-flecked formica and stainless steel, the *pièce de résistance* of which was a full-sized stand-up shower.

We went next into the main part of the cabin, which was several times as roomy as the main cabin of *Merrywend;* Poletti asked his son to get off the brocade-covered couch on the starboard side, so that he could show me how it unfolded to become a double bed. On the port side, opposite it, were white plastic-covered dinette benches at another formica-topped table, and on shelves, tables, and windowsills around the cabin were such pieces of bric-a-brac as a bowl containing wax fruit, two pottery pheasants, three dolphins, several Toby mugs, and a china flowerpot containing a green plastic philodendron. A portable television set was stowed on a forward bunk in a separate little cabin.

"We got just everything we need," said Poletti. "Electric

86

fan-operated heaters for when it gets cold. An electric auto-matic bilge pump in case we take any water. The exhaust fan. The pumps for running water. An electric percolator, even. And we've got plenty of power for when we need it. I can do twenty-five knots if I want to run away from a storm—I pity you sailboat fellows who have to sit out there and take it—but mostly I like to cruise slowly around little islands and bays just looking at things and taking it easy. It's the nicest way to relax I know of. And everything's made *right*, so we're as comfortable here as we are in our house.

"All three of us like to feel completely at home on a boat. We spend a lot of time on board during the summer—more than we do at home. We live in New Haven, but four days a week, all summer long, we're on the boat. We keep it about twenty-five miles from home, at a marina in a little Con-necticut harbor. Everybody on our dock is friendly and knows everybody else. It's like a neighborhood. Sailboaters don't understand that. They're always trying to prove some-thing, or test themselves, or see how much they can take. As for us, we like to take it easy, and move around and stay in a different port each weekend. We come up here to Green-port pretty often—I could make it in about an hour, but I take my time—and we know a lot of the other boat people here, which we like. We always spend two, three days here at a time. It's a great town—there are bowling alleys on the main drag, and a laundromat, and movies, and churches. What more does anybody else need? And you know what else is great about cruising?—you really learn to live with each other. On a boat you can't get away from each other. If you have a little spat, you have to fix it up and get over it. It's a good way to learn how to live with each other. It's together-ness." Poletti was so persuasive that I felt my sailboat insular-ity being genuinely imperiled; thanking him, I left this hotbed of contagion and made my way back to my own boat, to which Al and Geoffrey had preceded me.

On board, I decided to leave Greenport and find a quieter

place to spend the night. Less than a mile across the water lay Dering Harbor, scooped out of Shelter Island—a spot I was familiar with, because I had once spent a summer here. At 10 P.M., after studying the chart carefully and taking bearings, we turned on the running lights and the compass light, cast off, and motored slowly across. Midway, the maneuver began to seem more difficult than we had imagined; the night was moonless and extremely dark, and the few scattered lights on Shelter Island were more confusing than helpful. As we eased into the formless blackness of Dering Harbor, our binoculars showed us other boats as faint, dusky shapes on the black water. We proceeded at a crawl, with a good deal of urgent shouting back and forth between Geoffrey, on the bow, and me, at the wheel and throttle, until we finally seemed to be at the edge of a fleet of boats of about our own size. When I decided we were within the safe anchoring area but had enough space all around, I called for the anchor to be lowered away, and after checking our position for ten minutes or so, to see that we were neither dragging anchor nor swinging too close to the other boats, we considered ourselves at home for the night, and felt well pleased with ourselves for having groped our way in the dark into this calm, silent retreat.

Saturday, August 17

At 6:30 A.M., I looked out the companionway to see a large, half-flaccid red balloon of sun moving up from the horizon of trees and, as it floated free, growing round and too bright to look at. The first piece of business after breakfast was to restock the galley with food and buy certain other supplies, so around eight-thirty we motored back across the water to Greenport and tied up at the same big dock, where we took on gasoline, water, and ice. Next, we walked over to Main Street and visited the A&P, the drugstore, and a drygoods shop. In every port town all around Long Island Sound, from late spring to early fall, the observant passer-by can spot cruising people like ourselves on Main Street, dressed in sun-faded jeans or chinos, rubber-soled shoes, and visored caps, and carrying great bags full of food and drink back to their boats. At the upper levels of yachtsmanship, of course, one does not do so; the larger boats, especially those with paid crew—and John Scott-Paine told me he estimates there are at least a thousand boats on the Sound as large as *Florencia II* at Stamford Yacht Haven—have supplies either delivered to the dockside, or carried back by a deckhand. But then, the owners of such boats have crews to handle them, and do not even experience the sense of mastery sailors get on smaller craft; carrying one's own groceries seems to me a small price to pay.

Having brought a great load of things aboard and stowed them all away, we cast off at about 9:30 A.M. and began working our way back around Shelter Island and eastward along the inner shore of the North Fork toward Plum Gut. Last night, before going to sleep, we had consulted the *Tidal Current Tables* and *Tidal Current Charts* to see whether we would be able to sail back into the Sound through Plum Gut or would have to use the motor to push us through. A considerable part of the pleasure of sailing consists in doing by primitive means and with great difficulty what can be done easily and quickly by modern technology. A big Chris-Craft can zip through Plum Gut no matter which way the current is going, but a sailboat using only her sails must calculate everything to a nicety and then work hard. We had found that if we were careful to arrive at Plum Gut no later than 11 A.M., we would be sailing through it when only two knots of current were opposing us, and with any fair amount of wind we could manage this easily; toward noon the current would increase rapidly, and even with a favoring wind we might be unable to push through. In Plum Gut or The Race, indeed, it is possible to sail smartly backward—relative to the land—when the current is at its strongest.

We were fairly well into Plum Gut by ten-forty-five, with a steady, moderate wind from the southwest, which was ideal for getting us through under sail. Though the current was not yet strong, the flow of various waters through the passage was so complex that there were sharp tide rips; an area of roiled water and white breakers to our left ended along a line as clear-cut as though it had been drawn with a ruler. With a great deal of tacking and jibbing, we managed to avoid the tide rips and work the boat slowly through the passage; the current carried us sidewise, toward Plum Island, however, and though we cleared the island safely, we could not avoid a second rip, on this side of the passage. The boat lurched about in it miserably for some moments, battling a current that was trying to sweep us out into Block Island Sound; then, as we passed the western tip of Plum Island and entered the waters of Long Island Sound, we crossed a divide in the flow, and instantly we were out of the rip and in smooth, placid water, with the current flowing our way.

Now, as we took up our north-northeast course, Connecticut was faintly visible to our left as an accent on the horizon, and to our right, only a few hundred yards away, was Plum Island. Plum and three islands lying beyond it to the northeast in a straight line—Great Gull, Little Gull, and Fishers Island, across The Race—mark high points of the underlying ridge on which the glacial moraine that became Long Island was stranded. This means that Plum Island has the same shallow sand cliffs and beached rocks as the North Fork. About two and a half miles long, it is mostly green and wild-looking, so strangers are surprised to see, toward its southwest end, a sprawling, modern factory-type building and some associated structures. The big building is the Animal Disease Laboratory of the Department of Agriculture—the only place in the United States where foreign animal diseases are studied. Yachtsmen are not permitted to enter Plum Island's nearly landlocked harbor except in real emergencies, though there is no alternative harbor closer than Niantic Bay, in Connecticut, eight miles to the north. The scene all around us constituted an almost perfect example of the many facets of modern society exhibited by Long Island Sound. Next to us was forbidden Plum Island, its up-to-date laboratory building contrasting with its untamed greenery; behind us lay the mournful tip of Long Island, past which a large ferry loaded with cars and people on their way to or from a vacation was making its way from Connecticut; far down the Sound and fast disappearing in the light haze was the silhouette of a westbound freighter; to our left and ahead were some of the prime fishing grounds of the Sound, in which at least a score of private and chartered fishing boats were wallowing about, bristling with rods; through their midst a graceful black yawl was picking her way; and beyond them the long, ominous, cluttered shape of Navy Destroyer 695 was cutting swiftly northeast toward the smudgy profile of New London, on the far horizon.

From the eastern end of Plum Island to the tip of Fishers Island there stretch seven miles of virtually open water, Great Gull Island being only a snippet of land and Little Gull a scrap of rock. Between the latter and the near end of Fishers Island, which is known as Race Point, is a four-mile stretch of water, the deepest section of which, near Fishers Island, is The Race, the major opening between the Sound and the ocean. Back and forth through it, every six hours or so, passes most of that immense surge of water that partly drains and then refills Long Island Sound, lowering and raising its thousand or so square miles of surface by an average of some six feet, and drawing water out of or shoving it into every harbor, tidal pond, gunk hole, river, and creek all the way to

Throgs Neck. This great slosh travels through the Sound in slow motion, made slower in some places by accidents of geography or the flow of rivers, with the result that in certain bays high tide or the time of maximum current flow may be hours later than high tide or maximum current flow at The Race. Normally, the water rushing through The Race reaches a maximum velocity of about four knots, but when the moon is full, and the tides are at their highest and strongest, it can pour through at as much as six knots. Doubtless because of this violent sluicing back and forth, which must have occurred something like sixty million times since the Ice Age ended and the ocean rose to its present level, The Race has washed out to a depth of over three hundred feet in places, or several times the depth of the water anywhere around it for fifty miles.

Despite these extraordinary currents, sailing The Race is not as uncomfortable as sailing through the tide rips of Plum Gut. It does take even more forethought, though. On a hazy or rainy day, for instance, a careless mariner who heads across The Race without consulting the *Tidal Current Tables* and doing a little dead reckoning may be smoothly and imperceptibly swept sidewise out to sea at a rate of five or six knots while making only three knots forward. By the time he spots Fishers Island through the murky air or rain, he may be out in Block Island Sound, and if he does not have a direction-finding radio on board, he is likely to mistake Fishers Island for the Connecticut-Rhode Island coastline, and may sail blithely on into the open ocean, wasting hours, or perhaps even getting himself caught in the Atlantic during a storm, until, as Milton put it, his bones are hurled by the whelming tide to the bottom of the monstrous world. However, the presence of Race Rock Light, a sixty-seven-foot lighthouse perched on a rock a short distance off the western end of Fishers Island, is designed to prevent just such mistakes; it has a brilliant white-and-red flashing light, and also what the Coast Guard calls a "siren," which utters a periodic cowlike moo that can be heard for a considerable distance.

For some time, various committees of developers and engineers, both self-appointed and state-appointed, have urged putting a bridge across the open water of this untamed passage. As they envision it, the bridge would hop off at Orient Point, skip and jump across Plum and the two Gulls, make a mighty vault across The Race to Fishers Island, and then leap from its eastern end over to Watch Hill, on the mainland. It would actually be not so much a bridge as a twenty-three-mile chain of bridges, elevated roadways, causeways, and bits of highway. An impressive conception, no doubt, but, sitting at the wheel of my boat this fine day, with miles of ruffled blue water stretching out in all directions, the wind driving me along in a smooth, rolling motion, the deep, voiceless pouring of the tide beneath me, and the land only a faint gray-green promise on the horizon, I felt totally unsympathetic to the idea of any bridge. No matter how many millions of New Englanders and Long Islanders it would allow to drive into each other's territory, the price would be too high—the world would have been robbed of one more mystery, and one more part of the earth would have been humbled, domesticated, and safely tamed.

By 1 P.M., we had crossed The Race and were sailing close to Fishers Island, in a partly sheltered body of water, eight miles long and two miles wide, that is called Fishers Island Sound but, geologically speaking, is the eastern end of Long Island Sound. Its outer boundary, Fishers Island, is a wriggling piece of land, itself eight miles long, that lies roughly parallel to the mainland. (Though it is so near the Connecticut coast, it is officially a part of New York's Suffolk County.) Hilly and tree-covered, and with rocks on its beaches and its many promontories, it has a wildly romantic, legendary look about it, but we, because this was our first day in these waters, were more concerned with the Sound than with the island. Fishers Island Sound, roomy though it seems, is full of shallows, rocks, and islets; here one finds obstacles named North Dumpling and South Dumpling, West Clump, Middle Clump, and East Clump, Intrepid Rock, Flat Hammock, Eel Grass Ground, and the like. Clearly, it is no place for daydreaming sailors, and we paid close attention to the chart and the buoys until, opposite the eastern end of Fishers Island, we made our way between two breakwaters outside Stonington Harbor, on the Connecticut mainland, and dropped sail. We then motored a short distance up the harbor, and by 2:30 P.M. we were in a small marina called the Dodson Boat Yard, where we tied up in a slip assigned us by an attendant on the dock.

Here *Merrywend* had a change of crew. Al and Geoffrey packed their things, phoned for a cab, and left for New London, where they would catch a train for New York. After they had gone, I spent an hour or so working around the boat, and then luxuriated in a shower in a small building onshore. Toward 5 P.M., one of my two new crew members, an old friend named Mike Lanin, strolled jauntily down the dock, having just arrived from New York by train and cab. Not having cruised before, he seemed to have taken it for granted that *Merrywend* would be where I had said she would be, and on the right day. Actually, wind and weather being as quixotic as they are, every marina or harbor on Long Island Sound has impatient mariners fidgeting around it for days throughout the summer, waiting for friends whom they are expecting to join but who have been fogged in, turned back by storms, or delayed by motor trouble or lack of wind. The other member of the crew for the rest of the cruise would be a Harvard graduate student named Alan Fuchs, who was due to come down by train and bus from Cambridge and meet us the next day at Mystic.

After Mike had stowed his things and looked the boat over, we walked around the yard awhile. Dodson's is a modest-sized marina, with thirty-five slips at the docks and forty moorings out in the water. Today, it had a number of power-boats, several large and very sumptuous sailboats, and one huge houseboat, whose most notable features were jalousies, a back porch with garden furniture, and a large, fully furnished living room. Onshore were a ship's store, shower and toilet facilities, and a boathouse for repair work. This, evidently, was a mariner's marina, and not a country club. The owner, John Dodson, whom we found scrubbing the deck of a modest sloop of his own, proved to be a short, bony man in his early fifties wearing faded dungarees and with a face as spare and weathered as a New England hillside. He looked so much like an old salt that I assumed he had been a boatyard operator all his life, but he told me he had entered the marina business only in 1959. "I used to be a coal-mine operator in eastern Pennsylvania, but my people summered up here for many years, and ever since I was a child I've loved boats," he said. "Running a marina is wonderful—all it takes, during the summer, is fifteen hours of my time per day, seven days a week."

I asked what sort of people used his marina.

"We have real boat-loving people here," he said. "No partying, no showing off, very little living at the dockside. Our people want to get out on the water as soon as they're aboard. About half of them are fine old-line Stonington families, and the others are serious boat-lovers from miles around. There's really nothing to keep them here. No smart shops, no fine restaurants in Stonington; it's just an old fishing port, and a lot of its people are of Portuguese extraction. We seldom get the fancier transients, and if one does stray in, he takes a good look and clears out. We're really quite blessed here."

Bidding the beatified Mr. Dodson goodbye, we walked downtown to a seafood restaurant, where, over chicken lobsters, we discussed plans for the balance of the cruise. First, we decided, we would poke our way eastward for the final couple of miles and put into Little Narragansett Bay, the absolute end of the Sound, and then we would turn westward and work our way slowly along the Connecticut coast. I planned to spend a week covering the eighty-five miles between Little Narragansett and Stamford. Ordinarily, one could cruise that distance easily in three days, but there were many things I wanted to see along the way.

I was tired, and turned in early, but my night was not to be peaceful; a steady rain began falling at about 3 A.M., and since we were not at anchor, with the stern free to swing away from the wind, the rain drove down the open companionway into my face. I climbed into the upper bunk, and still I was rained on; finally, struggling up once more from the depths of sleep, I pulled on foul-weather gear, climbed up into the cockpit, and rummaged around in the storage compartments for the two boards that slide into the companionway to seal it shut. Back in my bunk, I found I was unable to get to sleep again, and fell to reviewing the last few years of my life. One is hardly ever as remote from the world as on board a boat tied up in a tiny harbor on the Sound—a situation that contributes most marvelously to perspective, especially at three o'clock of a rainy morning. One is able to see quite accurately all that has been distorted or out of proportion. Everything vexing, alarming, or momentous seems an ephemeral trifle. In the morning, alas, the momentousness of trifles returns, and the high resolve to live according to one's nighttime perspective is, unhappily, worn away by the seeming needs of each day.

Sunday, August 18

THIS WAS A SULLEN, DRIPPING MORNING with wet, woolly clouds smothering the land and sea. Every few minutes, Mike or I would go up on deck and peer at the sky, wondering whether it would clear later and give us a decent day. In New York, I am, like most people, only marginally aware of the weather. Before going out of my apartment, I want to know what the temperature is and whether it is raining, but I don't experience weather in any real sense; it is only an interim sensation, a transient state, known briefly between the enduring reality of interiors—living room, subway, stores, offices, the library. On the Sound, the situation is reversed; the sky and the air and the things they contain are the real world, and the interiors of boats and buildings are only burrows that one crawls into for brief periods to comfort oneself. The sailor is forever intensely aware of the sky, immense and enveloping. On the Sound, as on the open sea, one is in, under, and of the sky; one's eyes constantly search its vastness to know whether it means well or ill. When the sky changes, the man under it finds that his mood changes accordingly: sometimes it is infinitely roomy and pellucid, and then his soul is transparent and melodious; sometimes it is half opaque and sullen, its intent unclear, and then his mood is guarded, querulous, and doubting; sometimes it lies heavily upon him, suffocating him in its foggy embrace, or lashing him with a million angry little blows, and then his mood may be anything from dejected or grim to stoical or defiant.

Yet the moment he steps ashore, he becomes detached from the continuum. The sky is now a thing apart; he owns himself, the sky does not own him. The nearest doorway or store is his refuge from the indignities it may wish to inflict upon him, and his business is with other men under roofs, not under the bowl of earth's atmosphere. He enters the city, and no longer sees the dome of sky as the largest part of his world; it has been dismembered, humiliated, torn into shreds and scraps of background between the edges of buildings. The battalions of billowing cumulus he once saw marching in majestic order along the horizon, the pendulous rain clouds that scudded over the face of the earth, the high delicate tracery of cirrus clouds etched against the vault of blue, all are now sliced up and seen only as mean slivers of openness between man's works.

For us, in the Dodson Boat Yard, the sky was still our world, but, this morning, a distinctly unpromising one. On the basis of its looks and the weather report, we decided to wait awhile before putting out, and, with time to kill, we wandered off for a look at Stonington, which had been an important port for the cargo vessels of the eighteenth century and the whalers of the nineteenth. Only tight-lipped Puritans, probably, would ever have chosen to settle upon this stern fingerlike outcropping of sterile granite, yet the town itself has a surprising amount of charm—if more, perhaps, for a visiting antiquarian than for its inhabitants. Even on this dismal morning, we were delighted by the fine old houses, the white churches, the shade trees, and the waterfront, strewn with what almost seemed a set of theatrical props, including fishing boats, casks, nets, lobster traps, and coils of rope.

Stonington goes about its own business much as it has for centuries, and makes few concessions to the tourist; the principal one seemed to be the presence of hand-lettered signs nailed onto the authentic old houses, more or less identifying them, although the identification was sometimes no help whatever. A one-and-a-half-story Cape Codder on Main Street, for instance, bore the legend "Col. Oliver Smith 1761," but offered no clue as to who Colonel Smith had been. (He'd been a local shipbuilder, as I later learned.) Similarly, the sign on a red-shingled salt-box house grudgingly offered only the words "Elkanah Cobb House 1774." Elsewhere, though, someone had unbent a little more: on an imposing two-story yellow home in formal Georgian style was a sign saying "1700 A.D. Capt. Wm. Pendleton Master Mariner & Ship Owner," and on Water Street a Cape Codder bore the practically verbose sign "The Thomas Ash House 1700 Mr. Ash was a rope maker. His daughter opened a private school."

The rain that had been threatening now arrived. We hurried back to the boat, wet, chilly, and out of sorts—a condition we remedied with a tot of spirits and some hot clam chowder. We then felt so much better that we cast off at noon, wet and windy though it was, and hoisted sail in the harbor. To cover the one tiny remnant of Long Island Sound lying to the east of us, we headed around the breakwater and for a couple of miles followed the nuns and cans marking a channel in that direction. This led us through Little Narragansett Bay, a bleak bit of shallow water with a sandy islet on our right, over which gulls were wheeling and lamenting, and the low green line of the Rhode Island shore on our left. At the far end of the bay, we came upon a small marina, but didn't tie up there, being content to admire just in passing the brown-shingle-and-fieldstone mansions and the big yellow hotel on Watch Hill.

This being the very end of the Sound, we felt a little like Amundsen's party when, having reached the South Pole after prolonged efforts, they turned around and got out in a hurry. We swung smartly about and headed down the channel. By the time we were back in the deeper and roomier waters of Fishers Island Sound, the clouds were thinning rapidly, the sun was beginning to break through, and boats of all sorts were appearing everywhere. A number of them were heading southeast, through the passage between Fishers Island and Watch Hill, for the waters of Block Island Sound and the open Atlantic. Because we had plenty of time to spare—we were going to spend the night at Mystic Seaport, only a short distance down the coast—we, too, headed out that way, south of Watch Hill and outside the sheltered waters of Long Island Sound. I had hoped that out here, by way of contrast to the Sound, we might find the Atlantic swell, that long rolling movement of the water which can slowly and smoothly lift a boat ten or twenty feet, and then lower it again, without causing it to pitch or falter in its forward movement. But this day there was no swell, and perhaps it was just as well; Mike had not been on board a boat for some time, and when I merely described the swell with some enthusiasm, he blanched and popped a Bonamine into his mouth.

After an hour or so, we returned once more to Fishers Island Sound, this time via Watch Hill Passage and Napatree Point Ledge, and continued through it toward the mouth of the Mystic River, four miles to the west. Our course took us near the north side of hilly, irregular Fishers Island, which proved to have an untamed, Hebridean look about it; here and there a swath of lawn had been carved out of the trees, and on it stood some vast mansion or, once, a turreted castle, giving the island a fairy-tale quality. Halfway down Fishers Island Sound, we turned north into the Mystic River. In the days of sail, the Mystic was a major shipbuilding and shipping center, and though it is nothing of the sort any longer, its broad lower reaches are cluttered with boatyards for pleasure craft and with piers and dockside eating places, while fleets of powerboats and sailboats lie at moorings, and outside the channel are the rotting hulks of old workboats and sunken barges. Since Mystic Seaport lay two and a half miles upstream, we prudently dropped sail and started the motor as the river grew narrower and the channel traffic became heavier. In the old days, of course, the crews of even the largest whalers and coastwise schooners worked their way upstream under sail, but then they had no choice. Just before five o'clock, we passed through an open swing bridge of the New York, New Haven & Hartford Railroad and, a short distance ahead, saw a closed bascule bridge, over which a steady stream of cars was moving along U.S. Route 1. In the brief stretch of river between the two bridges, a dozen powerboats and sailboats were either circling slowly or lying by the wooden seawall and holding on; a sign announced that the bascule bridge would be opened at ten minutes past the hour and again at forty minutes past. We waited ten minutes, and at five-ten the barriers went down, traffic stopped, the bridge slowly floated upward, and all the waiting boats went through.

Rounding a bend a short distance ahead, we came upon a striking sight—a replica of a waterfront of a century or more ago. This was Mystic Seaport—one of those somewhat self-conscious artificial evocations of the past, like Williamsburg and Greenfield Village. It may be non-U of me, but I can't help being entranced by them, just as I can't help enjoying a well-reconstructed room of an earlier century in a museum. Lying before us was a panorama of piers and wharves over which towered the masts, yardarms, and weblike ratlines of several square-rigged sailing vessels. The curving, cobbled street along the waterfront was strewn with draymen's carts, hogsheads, anchors, and other contributions to a seaport *mise en scène*, and on the far side of the street were eighteenth- and nineteenth-century houses, sheds, and shops of wood and stone. There was no time to study all this at the moment, however. Instead, we headed for the longest wharf, which projected into the river, and there hailed the bronzed dock-master and told him we were *Merrywend;* since dock space is sometimes hard to come by at Mystic Seaport, I had written ahead for a reservation. He promptly waved us into a berth alongside his wharf. Standing beside him, and also waving, was Alan Fuchs, the remaining member of the crew for the rest of the trip. Alan grabbed the line we threw across, and very soon we had tied up, stepped onto the dock, and registered for the night, and were free to look around. To my delight, I found that we were at the same wharf as *Charles W. Morgan*, the last wooden whaling ship extant—a fat black hull over a hundred feet long, from which rose three giant masts, with three huge yardarms on each, and a great, mystifying web of rigging that made cats' cradles in the air high over the deck.

A while later, when we had got Alan's things stowed aboard, we walked along the waterfront to a shower room reserved for visiting yachtsmen; crowds of landlubbers were also walking along it, and they gawked at us as though we ourselves were from another century. When we had cleaned up and put on fresh clothes, we took a cab to a restaurant a few miles away, and by the time we got back, the daytime tourists had all left; aside from guards and a number of teen-agers receiving mariner training aboard two permanently moored square-riggers, the only people who ever inhabit Mystic Seaport at night are a few score visiting yachtsmen like us. Mystic Seaport, though it has been put together with loving verisimilitude, is a synthetic village and has no residents. Each house, shop, and artifact in it is authentic, but practically everything has been brought here from somewhere else, to occupy a place assigned it by a street plan that is the imaginative work of contemporaries. In essence, Mystic Seaport is an outdoor museum. As such, it is unique, being the only museum to which people can come in their own boats— and a fair number of the cruising boats one sees in eastern Long Island Sound on any given day during the summer either are heading for or have just left Mystic Seaport. There is space enough at the wharves of Mystic Seaport for about forty-five pleasure boats, and twice that number can be accommodated by the device of rafting, or tying a second boat alongside one that is made fast to the dock. Between April and October, approximately three thousand boats, bringing approximately ten thousand visitors, come to Mystic Seaport, some from distant points. This is only a tiny fraction of the total attendance—in 1962, for instance, 304,000 people visited the place, all except the ten thousand making the trip by land—but the yachtsmen add more to the nautical flavor of the scene than their numbers might suggest. For their part, they have the heady privilege of owning the village overnight, when the day people are shooed out and the gates are locked. So it was with us. When we returned from dinner, we wandered around the streets by the light of electrified whale-oil lamps, feeling not quite firmly anchored in our own century, but transported backwards in time. Our feet scuffed the dust, or felt the rounded cobblestones, of the old streets down which we walked, and we could all but hear the feet of men of

1830 or 1840 scuffing along ahead of us. Cluttered heaps of iron staves and spoked wheels lay alongside the ironmonger's shop, and it seemed as though surely he had only gone home an hour or two ago to have his roast beef and his pint, and would be back in the morning. Through the countinghouse window we could see the ledger open as it had been during the day's work, the writing shaded and graceful with many a fine flourish, but the clerk had gone, perhaps to prayer meeting. The apothecary, too, must be home dining, or already in his four-poster bed, but in his shop window were flasks and jars of medicine for our disorders; on the morrow, if we required it, he would dispense us medicaments compounded of "Essent. Sassafras," "Aeth. Sulphur," "Spiritus Lavandulae," and the like. Past *Charles W. Morgan* we walked, on our way back to our own boat, and looked up at the ratlines and the crow's nest dim against the night sky, wondering about the men who could climb up there above a wildly rolling sea, in a howling Antarctic gale, clinging with legs and body while using their hands to furl the sails. So we finally came back to our own time, for, having thought of those sailors and their hardships, we longed for our own warm bunks aboard *Merrywend,* and gratefully tumbled into them, content with the evils of our own day and unwilling to exchange them for those of any other.

Monday, August 19

B<small>Y</small> 6 A.M., I WAS UP AND DRESSED and walking down Seaport Street, along the waterfront. The dawn was clear, but, mid-August or not, the temperature was in the fifties. Mist drifted over the river, the cobblestones under my feet were slippery, and the small houses and shops were half hidden by a light ground fog. All this, plus the fact that no one else seemed to be up, wonderfully heightened the illusion of the place. It was an ideal time to wander around the town, looking at the things men had used and lived by: the little wooden cases full of type in the print shop; the scores of long-handled iron adzes, chisels, and other tools in the shop of A. W. Burrows, Shipwright; the compasses, nets, lanterns, and other gear in a window under the sign "Ship Chandlery—N. F. Fish, Prop." Later in the day, all these places would be oc-cupied. About forty elderly people from the nearby town of Mystic work for the Seaport, each day putting on mid-nine-teenth-century costume and playing their parts in the various buildings: the printers make shift to look as if they are print-ing (and do occasionally turn out a few samples), the black-smith lights and frequently rakes a smoky fire, though he does very little hammering, the countinghouse proprietor explains things to visitors but counts no money, and the bartender at the tavern stands behind the bar but dispenses only water. All this is entertaining, though a bit on the Disneyland side; I preferred the misty solitude of early morning, in which every-thing seemed far more real to me than it did later on when buildings were occupied by the costumed "activists." Why anyone gave the elderly amateur actors this dreadful name I cannot imagine, but semantics are a problem in a place like Mystic Seaport. What, for that matter, *is* Mystic Seaport? Not a restoration, and not even a duplication, since the town never existed as such. Mrs. Alma Eschenfelder, publicity director for Mystic Seaport, whom I met later this morning, told me, "We prefer to call Mystic Seaport a *re-creation*," but even this seems not quite right; a "creation" would be closer to the fact. There was, and still is, a real town called Mystic nearby, but Mystic Seaport is something else. The twenty-seven-acre tract upon which it is built was, for many years, the site of the George Greenman & Bros. Shipyard, and only two or three buildings in the present town stood here prior to 1929. At that time, three local history buffs—a doctor, a lawyer, and a businessman—got the idea of creating Mystic Seaport by hunting down and assembling specimens of eighteenth- and nineteenth-century New England seaport architecture, boats, and artifacts. They formed the nonprofit Marine Historical Association, and started raising money, soliciting gifts of property, and putting things together; since then, several dozen buildings, scores of boats, and innumerable artifacts have been gathered together here and are worth about three million dollars in the aggregate.

On my way back to *Merrywend*, I passed by *Xiuhcoatl*, a Rhodes Woodpussy (a fourteen-foot day-sailer) that was tied up next to us at our wharf, and heard a hearty sneeze resound under the tarpaulin cover stretched over it. In a moment, a corner was peeled back and the tousled head of a young man emerged. We greeted each other and traded names (his was Anthony Reveaux), and I expressed surprise that he had slept in his cockpit, which not only is no longer than a big bathtub, but has a centerboard trunk—a kind of vertical partition— sticking up, right in the middle of it. Reveaux amiably replied that he was perfectly comfortable in it; he inflated a plastic mattress at night, wriggled into a sleeping bag, and did not in the least mind the tightness, bounciness, or chill of his bedroom. Reveaux courageously undertook extended cruises in his little day-sailer; he lives in Stony Creek, near New Haven, and this visit to Mystic Seaport was the high point of a five- or six-day trip. I asked him about the practical problems of single-handed cruising in such a boat. He carried no motor, he told me, but depended entirely on wind and currents; accordingly, he sometimes had to spend as much as fourteen hours alone at the tiller. While holding it with one hand all day long, he would now and again make shift with the other hand to fish out some food from a plastic bag, pour water for himself from a jug, use a saucepan for necessary relief, and tune in weather forecasts on a small portable radio. Some nights he would tie up in a harbor like Mystic Seaport, where he could wash and go to a restaurant; other nights he would anchor or moor where there were no accommodations, and would have to use a bit of his drinking water for washing and cook his dinner, out of cans, over a tiny alcohol stove which he kept stowed under the bow. One would ordinarily expect such prodigies of self-mortification only in a proselytizing health-and-strength fanatic, but Reveaux, who is a planning aide in the New Haven Redevelopment Agency, spoke of his sailing in a modest, half-apologetic, and quite disarming manner. I have seen hundreds of day-sailers frisking about on the Sound over the years, without ever supposing that any of them might be engaged in so ambitious an activity as this, and once again I was bemused by the variety of ways in which men use and enjoy the Mare Internum.

Mike, Alan, and I spent the morning sight-seeing in Mystic Seaport, along with the flocks of visitors who poured in through the gates from nine o'clock on. After lunch, we cast off and proceeded under power down to the highway bridge, just in time to be let through. The afternoon was benign and sunny, with a mild, steady wind that was ideal for training a couple of new hands. (I had given Mike some, but not enough, instruction the previous day, and Alan had had none, his only sailing experience being on tiny catboats on the Charles River, in Cambridge.) We spent the next few hours in and around Fishers Island Sound; I lay back on a pile of cockpit cushions, beer can in hand, and gave orders while Mike and Alan learned how to sail the boat first close-hauled, then on a beam reach, and finally running, and practiced coming about, jibbing, and heaving to.

By five o'clock, we had put in a good afternoon's work, so we headed inside the Dumplings, by way of a marked channel, for West Harbor, on Fishers Island. This is a pocket of water three quarters of a mile wide tucked into the low green hills at the western end of the island. There was a small marina, at which forty or fifty powerboats were tied up, but we chose to drop anchor amid a couple of dozen boats moored out in the water. Hardly anywhere in the Sound—not even at the Seawanhaka-Corinthian Yacht Club, in Oyster Bay—does one see a more impressive or cosmopolitan group of sailboats than here; poor *Merrywend* was dwarfed and shamed by the company she was keeping. The home ports of the other visitors ranged from New York to Seattle, and the finest of the lot was a huge, sleek white ketch with towering masts, scrupulously gleaming metalwork, mirrorlike varnish on her cabin, and a maze of lines and special gear whose uses we could only guess at. Her name was *Barlovento II*, and as soon as we were safely anchored, I went below and looked her up in our invaluable *Lloyd's Register of American Yachts;* her owner proved to be Pierre du Pont and her designer the famous Philip Rhodes, and she was listed as nearly seventy-two feet in length and eighteen feet in beam. Side by side with her were three other sailboats, nearly as magnificent: *Maruffa*, a sixty-seven-foot yawl owned by John Graham, of Seattle; *Enchanta*, a sixty-six-foot yawl owned by Richard Stiegler, of Greens Farms, Connecticut; and *Seaflower*, a fifty-five-foot ketch owned by Steven M. Castle, of Stonington. Only Mr. du Pont's name was familiar to me, and I came to the conclusion that the United States has many well-to-do people of whom the non-well-to-do are virtually unaware. Perhaps it is better that way, for both sides.

Once we had taken in all this splendor, we concluded that there must be something special about Fishers Island—something neither shown on the charts nor explained in Duncan and Blanchard's *A Cruising Guide to the New England Coast*, which had been our handbook on this trip. Hoping to find out what it might be, we washed, dressed, rowed ashore in the dinghy (a neighboring boat had told us that there was no launch service after 7 P.M.), and made our way down a winding road, past scattered houses and then through a schoolyard, to the Pequot Inn. (Why "Pequot" I cannot figure out; my reading, perhaps imperfect, leads me to believe that the

Pequot Indians lived on the mainland, rather than on Fishers Island, and that the civilized Englishmen and Colonials, plus some friendly Indians, burned six or seven hundred of them alive in their stockade near Mystic in 1637.) This pleasant old hostelry, which has a garden, a cocktail lounge, and a restaurant, was quite deserted except for a waitress, a bartender, and a lady pianist, who was offering a mélange of Broadway show tunes and sentimental lieder such as "Nur Wer die Sehnsucht Kennt." Since things were so quiet this evening, the waitress, a pleasant little woman, was willing enough to chat. Fishers Island, she told us, had only about six hundred year-round residents, practically all of whom lived in Fishers Island Village, where we now were. Most of the adults were suppliers, contractors, or servants of the wealthy owners of the mansions we had seen elsewhere on the island. Yachts from all over would sometimes arrive by the dozen in West Harbor on summer weekends, but their crews never went any farther ashore than the village. Occasionally, the Pequot Inn would be jam-packed with them, plus a few people from the mainland and some newcomers who had built small houses on the western end of the island. By and large, however, Fishers Island, despite its closeness to so many major eastern cities, had not become a summer resort. Instead, it had remained primarily the private preserve of the owners of the baronial estates making up most of the island. While the waitress was getting our appetizers, Mike slipped out to the pay phone and brought back the local telephone book, which was the size of the *Reader's Digest*, though only a quarter as thick. We scanned the names, and amused ourselves by compiling a list of those that sounded like the landed gentry. No doubt we missed many, but even so, it was an impressive little list: Lammot, Pierre S., Reynolds, and Willis H. du Pont; Roger S. Firestone; Grant G. Simmons; George E. Roosevelt; Joseph S. Frelinghuysen; French Frick; and Screven Lorillard. We enjoyed a competent dinner, though I could not help wondering why Fate had assigned me a name and station so out of keeping with my just desires, which were to live like, and among, the barons of Fishers Island, and while rowing back to the boat in our dinghy, I kept hearing in my mind's ear, as though it were a musical theme, the words of a favorite stanza of mine from *Miniver Cheevy:*

> Miniver loved the Medici,
>   Albeit he had never seen one;
> He would have sinned incessantly
>   Could he have been one.

I rather doubt that the aristocrats of Fishers Island sin incessantly, but if they are not real Medici, I fear I am sometimes a real Miniver.

Tuesday, August 20

At 2 A.M., A VIOLENT BOOM OF THUNDER AWOKE ME. The wind was flinging handfuls of rattling rain at the cabin roof, and *Merrywend* was rocking up and down and swinging slowly from one side of her anchor line to the other. I peered out at the few lights on land for a while, checking our position, and looked for the faint night lights tied on the forestays of the boats anchored near us. Despite the fury of the wind, we seemed to be holding our place—largely, no doubt, because the bottom of West Harbor is satisfactorily muddy. Mariners on Long Island Sound get to know the consistency of the bottom of each of their favorite anchorages; indeed, such information is often indicated on the charts and in the *Cruising Guide*. Muddy bottoms are the safest, for they hold a dug-in anchor firmly; hauling it up in the morning, though, is likely to be a backbreaking job and a filthy one, since the anchor brings great gobs of sticky black mud up onto the deck with it. Sandy bottoms yield a clean anchor in the morning but do not offer as sure a hold against the yanking and straining that the anchor line undergoes when a powerful wind is blowing. Pebble or gravel bottoms, which are to be found in a few places, are a real hazard. The anchor can pull out of such material again and again, perhaps digging in by itself afterward, each time, only to pull out once more, and thus in the course of a night a boat can slowly and gently work its way across a bay. The members of its crew may sleep peacefully until they suddenly fall out of their bunks because their boat has landed on a mud bank and rolled over with the ebbing tide—or, worse yet, they may be awakened by the horrifying crunch of the hull upon rocks and the sound of the sea flooding into the bilge.

As I climbed back into my bunk, lightning flashed directly overhead and a great clap of thunder shook our cabin. Mike asked me in a thick mumble how things were, and I quoted him a line by George Herbert: "He that will learn to pray," I said, "let him go to sea." There was no answer but stertorous breathing, and I was obliged to chuckle alone at my sally. In the morning, a steady rain was falling. We were not eager to get wet, but after consulting the *Tidal Current Tables* we realized that unless we passed The Race before noon, we would be sailing westward quite near it at a time when the ebb current, outward bound, was rising toward four knots. Against that, even with a favoring wind, we would hardly be able to make good our westward course for Old Saybrook, at the mouth of the Connecticut River, but instead would be swept sidewise out of the Sound, winding up on the wrong side of Plum Island. We therefore reluctantly broke out the foul-weather gear after breakfast and emerged into the rain with an air of stern resolution. Actually, I think we all rather looked forward to being forced to get wet; most of the pleasure-boat mariners I have met enjoy minor discomforts like being wet or cold. They resist them, complain about them, and yet somehow like them when they happen. However, while we were still hauling up our mud-heavy anchor and hoisting the mainsail the rain diminished to a heavy mist, and within fifteen minutes even this had ended, though the leaden clouds never cleared away and the air remained soupy.

In a light but steady wind, we sailed close-hauled, passing between the Dumplings, on our right, and Fishers Island, on our left. Soon we could vaguely see Race Rock Light and hear its throaty siren. Ahead lay the whole length of Long Island Sound, the Connecticut shore green and indented, the Long Island shore straight and barren—or so I was able to imagine them from the previous days of observation. Today, the air, muffled by clouds and smeary with humidity, made each shoreline only a dark blur along the horizon. Quite near us on our right we could see the broad harbor mouth of the Thames River, and with the binoculars we could make out the smoke-stacks and buildings of Groton, on its east bank. As we were looking at these, Mike spotted the long malevolent shape of a submarine a mile or two ahead of us, rising to the surface and heading in toward the Thames. It looked like one of the new nuclear models to us. The Sound, which is so many things to so many people, is to submariners a test-and-training area. Nuclear submarines are built and launched in Groton, at the Electric Boat Division of the General Dynamics Corporation, and perform some of their initial test runs in the waters of the Sound between Niantic Bay and Plum Island; for deeper and more extended tests they go out through The Race into Block Island Sound and the Atlantic. Submariners in training at the New London naval base, across the Thames River from Groton, also use the eastern end of the Sound for some of their practice cruises, and the Coast and Geodetic Survey charts show their operating areas, outlining them in purple or red, and warning mariners to "proceed with caution" there and to stay away from naval target vessels flying large red flags. Under an often innocent-looking surface, the waters of the Sound hide a variety of hazards; besides submarines, there are undersea telephone cables that can foul one's anchor, sunken wrecks, shoals, rocks, fish traps, and rocky or hard bottoms where one cannot safely anchor. All these except the fish traps are shown on the more detailed charts, though.

Beyond Groton and New London, the coastline again became more typical of the eastern end of the Sound—green and peaceful, with scattered houses and brief strips of beach. The intrusions of mankind upon this coastline are an irregular intermingling of smudgy factory towns and quiet old fishing and farming villages. The latter are changing rapidly. During the summer I had visited several such towns and been told by the most knowledgeable people I could find—usually the local barber and the grocer—that city people were building summer homes around the outskirts of their town, developing the beaches, and turning the area into a summer resort, or even an all-year bedroom town for some nearby city. (Ever since the Connecticut Turnpike opened up along the shore, everything has been nearby everything else.) The local people are quite ambivalent about these changes: they like the business and the money the city people bring, but their hard-scrabble New England souls are contemptuous of, and offended by, the colorful cabañas, modern picture-window homes, art movies, nonobjective art, tipped hair, toreador pants, and restaurants with cocktail pianists.

The wind had died away almost to a dead calm, the water was gelatinous and slimy, and we could now see only about half a mile in any direction. Before long, we encountered an example of a bizarre phenomenon that sometimes occurs on the Sound under such conditions. The sailboat mariner, drifting along slowly, hears the far-off thrum of some unseen powerboat a mile or more away; then the sound recedes into the distance and is forgotten. Five or ten minutes later, a long, undulant line appears on the water some hundreds of yards off and rolls slowly toward him, eventually reaching him and rocking his boat about for a moment or two, much to his surprise. This is the wake of the powerboat, and such a wake can travel a surprisingly long way over calm water without being dissipated.

Because the weather was dispiriting and the boat all but inert until we started up our motor, the sixteen miles from West Harbor to the mouth of the Connecticut River seemed a great distance. Actually, we reached the entrance to the river before 4 P.M. The mouth of the Connecticut is quite broad, but there are a couple of large areas of submerged delta there, which would make it quite tricky except that at the western side of it there is a dredged and marked channel. This is both wide and deep, being designed to handle the commercial traffic that goes forty miles up the river to Hartford. Twin breakwaters outline the channel, and a fifty-eight-foot lighthouse on one of them monotonously utters a long, deep hoot somewhat like that of an ocean liner. Up the channel we proceeded, into the broad lower reaches of the river. A heavily loaded tanker pushed swiftly past us on its way to the interior of Connecticut, its deep wake rolling us about insanely. Fourteen hundred such tankers come here from the western end of the Sound every year, bringing central Connecticut most of its fuel oil and gasoline.

Some miles up the river are several places that are favorites with cruising yachtsmen, including the mint-condition eighteenth-century town of Essex and the isolated primitive inlet called Hamburg Cove. I had visited both in previous years, and while I had enjoyed them, this time I wanted to investigate the marina called Terra Mar, at Old Saybrook, just a mile inside the breakwaters. I had been told that it outdid even the Club Capri, in Port Washington, though I found this hard to believe. We now saw Terra Mar ahead of us on the west bank; its presence was attested by a large red neon sign and a neighboring modern-style hotel, all balconies and brightly enameled wall panels. A long wooden breakwater sheltered the marina from the flow of the river and the wakes of the tankers; a wide opening in the breakwater gave us access to the docks.

Until we had completed the ticklish job of maneuvering *Merrywend*, with her feeble single screw, into a narrow slip, to which the dockmaster assigned us, and had set out mooring lines fore and aft, we had no time to look about and see what kind of place we were in. At last, though, we were free to punch open three cans of cold beer and sit back to take stock of our surroundings. Terra Mar seemed much smaller than the Club Capri—we presently found out that it had only seventy-seven slips, to the Capri's two hundred-odd—but in some ways it was even plushier and even less nautical. The multi-colored hotel was not a neighboring property but a part of the marina complex, though it was separately owned; it catered to those cruising transients who preferred land-based bedrooms to their own cabin-cruiser staterooms, and to those permanent clients of Terra Mar who invited groups of friends down to sit on the boat for a weekend, or even go out for a short ride, but had no place to put them up. On the shore near the dock area were not one but three swimming pools— one for children to wade in, one for divers, and one for swimmers. There was also, of course, a good deal of poolside space for those who chose neither to wade nor dive nor swim but, rather, to play canasta and lie in the sun. On the docks, a couple of women in high heels clip-clopped along on their way to the cocktail lounge and restaurant, leaving behind on their boats a couple of maids, one of them looking after two children and the other putting leashes on a brace of poodles preparatory to taking them for a walk onshore. Dogs are so much a part of the boating scene at Terra Mar that the marina's printed rules and regulations, handed out to every slip-owner and transient, specify that the animals must be kept under control at all times, and add politely but firmly, "Should the size or temperament of your dog disturb the peace of others, the management reserves the right to cancel dockage."

After showering onshore, we ambled around the docks and made note of the mores of modern marina life. A medium-sized cabin cruiser named *Mystery II* had a standard housetop television antenna screwed onto a bollard at its slip; a wire ran from the cabin of the boat and was plugged into a lead from this antenna. *Lady Ann III*, a large, well-appointed yacht from Los Angeles, had white iron garden furniture on its open rear deck; on its forward deck was an anchor just like the one we had been using, but beautifully enameled in white and virginally innocent of any signs of service (in fact, no anchor line was attached to it, though I like to assume there was one around somewhere). The saloon of *Zarson,* an ocean-going yacht as big as any pleasure boat we had seen on the Sound thus far, was furnished elegantly, the high point being a full-sized spinet in its main saloon, though it lacked the ultimate touch of luxury we had seen in Fishers Island on Roger S. Firestone's new power cruiser, *Tireless*—original oil paintings on the walls.

We made for the bar, where a pianist was playing and well-dressed barflies had already foregathered. I fell into conversation with one marina employee, who shall remain nameless, and who, in answer to my question as to how much actual sailing these people did, said, "Frankly, most of our people aren't sailors at all. Of all our boatowners, I'd say only a dozen are real yachtsmen who know what they're doing and like going out on the water. The rest hardly ever cast off their mooring lines all season. Why should they? Everything they like is right here. There's even a combo and name entertainment in the dining room on weekends. A boat is a summer place to them, and a possession to be proud of. They *play* boat, they don't go boating. When they want to feel real nautical, they flip the switch to turn on the electric bilge pump, or run up their motors for a few minutes."

After dinner in the restaurant—which, far from making any pretense of being a mariners' eating place, had red-jacketed waiters, deep carpeting, and fancy chandeliers—we took one last snooping walk around the docks in the dark. On one boat a nonstop cocktail party was still in progress; on another, dinner for six was being served by a maid in white; elsewhere, card games were under way, families were watching television, and children in pajamas were resisting the idea of bed.

Wednesday, August 21

THE PLAN THIS DAY was to make an easy twenty-mile straight run along the shore to the Thimbles, a cluster of tiny islands lying off the village of Stony Creek, eight miles east of New Haven, though in doing so we would be passing right by at least three of my favorite places for spending the night: Duck Island Roads, a lonely offshore anchorage created by two long rock breakwaters; Clinton Harbor, an old New England town with a quiet and pleasant marina; and Guilford, another old New England town, with some particularly handsome eighteenth-century salt-box houses. The Connecticut shore offers the admirer of Colonial towns a rich selection—at the moment, that is, for they may soon disappear under a flood of shopping centers, drive-in movies, and modern office buildings—and the visitor gets a better view of the towns when he comes by boat than when he drives, simply because a mariner ashore is a pedestrian, and proceeds at a leisurely pace as he goes about seeking supplies and services, while the average motorist rushes in, pulls up near some famous building or other, stares at it through the car window, and then rushes back to the highway.

We had already spent some time in old towns, however, so right now I was more interested in the Thimbles, which had been strongly recommended to me by the owner of *Merrywend*. Twenty miles is not much, and, on a good day, ought to be no more than a four- or five-hour sail, but the current would help us only until 12:30 P.M., and by 1:30 P.M. would be a distinct hindrance, so an early start was in order. Unfortunately, the morning was foggy and we could see no farther than the nearest channel marker in the river. We therefore followed a procedure that is followed all summer long by innumerable mariners, not to mention sun worshippers and fishermen: we looked up at the sky every ten minutes and announced with conviction that the fog would burn off inside an hour. This time estimate is usually incorrect, but since fog almost always does burn off sooner or later, the prophet can see his prediction justified eventually if only he makes it often enough. Today, as it happened, the fog did burn off early; the blue began appearing directly overhead before 10 A.M., and a few minutes later, having paid our bill, we moved into the river under power and hoisted sail.

Outside the breakwaters, the visibility was fair, and we set course for the Thimbles, on a starboard tack. A light but steady wind from the north made us glide as evenly over the smooth water as if we were on a pond. It was a day of changeless, trancelike sailing, suspending us in a warm, thoughtless lethargy. The light wind was so steady and we had trimmed the sails to so nice a balance of pressures upon the boat that we could let the wheel alone for a whole minute at a time. The heat of the sun, combined with the haze, which made the details of the shore vaporous and unimportant, and the absence of other boats on the water, caused the day to slip by in a dream. In our half-asleep state, the pastel scenes and the names came and went, blended and overlapped. There were tree-clothed promontories venturing out into the sea from the rolling green countryside—Cornfield Point, Old Kelsey Point, Hammonasset Point, Sachem Head. There were harbors and gently concave bays between the points, each with its strip of pale beach, its scattered mansions, and its little cluster of summer cottages—Westbrook Harbor, Duck Island Roads, Clinton Harbor, Joshua Cove. There were islands, some of them mere craggy peaks awash, some of them long sandspits covered with pale-green salt grass, and some of them more substantial and boasting houses, bushes, and wind-twisted trees—Hen and Chickens, Halftide Rock, Salt Island, Menunketesuck Island, Duck Island, Halfacre Rock, Outer White Top, Falkner Island. There were towns, half guessed-at in the golden haze from a glimpse of roof, a water tower, a wisp of smoke, or a church spire—Westbrook, Clinton, Madison, East River, Guilford. And there was an almost unbroken string of summer communities on the water's edge, their roofs and windows glinting now and again in the sun. Only occasionally did we see things on the water itself—a faraway, ghostly-looking tanker, a small open boat into which three men were silently and doggedly hauling up lobster traps by hand, a soundless sailboat or two, a distantly throbbing power-boat. We spoke little, and needed little speech; we were at peace, understanding each other and all mankind; we were, for the time being, remade in a kindlier and nobler image of ourselves.

At last, there appeared, rising out of the water ahead and seeming to float upon it, a little flotilla of green blobs, which, as we drew closer, turned out to be trees growing on slabs of white granitic rock. These slabs were the Thimbles—a tiny archipelago resulting from the partial drowning by the Sound of several folded ridges of granite. The islets lie mostly in three closely spaced rows running northeast to southwest, the northeasternmost being less than a mile offshore. How many there are in all is not certain. The Chamber of Commerce of Branford, the town with jurisdiction over them, speaks of thirty islands, or about as many as a detailed chart gives names to, taking no account of scores of minor rocks; they range from substantial little domains of ten or twenty acres down to flat shards of granite a tenth of a mile or less in length. About a score of the larger islands have houses on them, in styles anywhere from the severely modernistic to quasi mansions in the Tudor and Georgian modes. No less welcoming terra firma was ever built upon by men. Even those islands which have some greenery have at best a mere film or thin carpet of earth made up of rotted mulch that has collected in hollows and crevices, while on several of the tinier islands, houses have been resolutely anchored upon uncompromisingly bald, sterile granite with nothing but perhaps a valiant few blades of grass or lichens living in a crack of the rock.

The names of the islands offer many a delight, and on the detailed chart I was happy to find, along with such insipid specimens as Smith, Davis, and High islands, more flavorful fare such as Mermaid Rock, Dogfish Island, Money Island (Captain Kidd is said to have buried treasure here), East Stooping Bush Island, Old Cobble Rocks, East Crib, West Crib, and, loveliest of all, Cut-in-Two Island. At about three o'clock we rounded the outermost of the Thimbles, straightforwardly named Outer Thimble, and could look down an avenue of water perhaps two hundred yards wide between two rows of the larger islands. In here, between Money Island and West Crib, the *Cruising Guide* promised a pleasant and sheltered place to anchor. We dropped our genoa, glided in slowly on the mainsail alone, rounded up into the wind between Money Island and West Crib, and there dropped the mainsail and let go the anchor. Though a friend and the *Cruising Guide* had told us to come here, we felt as though we had discovered the Thimbles; not another boat was to be seen at the moment, though on weekends, I'd been told, a score or more might anchor here overnight. All around us, nearby and far off, lay islands, some mere granite outcroppings and others covered with trees and shrubs. Most of them were untamed-looking, even when a house or two had managed to find a toehold upon them, but the one nearest to us—Money Island, about a hundred yards to the southeast—had homely little wooden houses practically cheek by jowl all along the shoreline overlooking our anchorage. In this idyllic setting, even those houses had a kind of pert winsomeness, perched defiantly and illogically, as they were, on a great slab of rock topped with trees.

Toward sundown, the weather being warm and sunny, and the water around us clear and flowing, we got into bathing suits and went over the side. While we were in the water, it occurred to me that we might swim over to Money Island and try wading ashore. The Thimbles are private property, and yachtsmen are not welcomed when they try to tie up there and go ashore, but I felt that swimmers might get a kinder reception. So we swam across, crawled cautiously up sloping rocks covered with tiny barnacles, and walked across a border of rough grass toward the row of houses. Mike, who had attended an all-night party on Money Island when he was an undergraduate at Yale, asked a man painting a wooden walkway where the McCammond house was. The painter didn't know, but an elderly couple, having overheard us, popped out of a nearby house and began to chat with us about the McCammonds, who had sold their house years ago. They introduced themselves as Mr. and Mrs. Leslie Coley, and seemed very willing to answer all my questions about the Thimbles, but since it was time for Mrs. Coley to be starting supper, she suggested we come back at about 6:30 P.M. This invitation made it legitimate for us to row over and tie up at the dock later on, and we thanked her and swam back to the boat. I heated water, shaved, and dressed, while Mike and Alan went off in the dinghy to visit aboard a large sloop that had anchored not far from us, with whose skipper they had struck up a conversation. Clean, deliciously tired, and perfectly contented, I sat in the cockpit with a long Scotch and water, my notebook at my side; my notes indicate a degree of euphoria I have known relatively few times in my life:

5:45 P.M. Sitting alone in cockpit. Mike and Alan visiting nearby Sparkman and Stephens sloop chartered by a man from New Hope, Pa. Sun westering in golden bowl of sky beyond East and West Cribs, light breeze cooling my cheeks, dog earnestly barking on nearby island, gulls crying somewhere. Water now almost mirror-like, islands seeming to float on it. Far away, by East Crib, a few people rowing and fooling about in boats. "Absolutely nothing half so much worth doing as simply messing about in boats." (Look this up—*Wind in the Willows*?) What could be finer than this? Who could be happier than I, though he dwelt in marble halls?

At 6:30 P.M. Mike and I left Alan writing a long letter, and rowed to the dock at the north end of Money Island. There are several rows of houses on the island, separated by broad avenues of native rock and grass, but we located the Coley house without trouble and were welcomed by Mr. Coley, a dignified clean-featured man who looked like a retired executive or banker, but had actually been a brass-factory foreman in Waterbury, Connecticut. He took us on a leisurely tour of the island, walking slowly and with a cane because of arthritis. "We've got thirty houses—more than any other island in the Thimbles," he said. "We run the island like a private club, through an association of property owners. Money Island belonged to the government until a fellow named Colonel Dickerson bought it, more than seventy-five years ago, and cut it up into lots. Wasn't much of anything here then except a few fishing shacks. Most of the houses and improvements have gone up since I started coming here, fifty years ago. We're still very much an island; we don't have electricity, and most of us use kerosene lamps for our light and compressed gas for our stoves and refrigerators. We get our drinking water from just one well—that's it over there, in that little open area. It's thirty feet deep. Where the fresh water comes from I don't know. You'd think the rain that falls on this rock would run right off, but I guess a lot filters down through the crevices into some kind of soil below. We have cisterns to catch rain water off our roofs for washing, and most of us use little one-cylinder gasoline engines to pump sea water up for our toilets. Over there is one of our two telephone booths. Several people have private lines now, but the rest of us rely on the booths. There's a button-and-buzzer system, so whoever answers the phone can signal around the island for the party that's wanted. See that funny-looking gray house? That's the McCammond place you were asking about. It used to be a dance hall long ago. A boat from New Haven used to bring people out on Sundays, and they'd have a gay time. But then the island gradually became a family place. We prefer it that way."

While Mr. Coley talked, I had been noticing the ingenious way in which people had tailored their houses to the rugged granite. The porch of the McCammond house was typical. It had been fitted around an upthrust finger of rock, the floor running up to the rock and surrounding it, so that the rock became a porch ornament. Elsewhere, houses were perched on sloping slabs of granite, or cantilevered out from them, or molded to the shape of the rock backing them. Couples sat on some of the porches, children raced up and down between the houses, and in one back yard a group of people were standing around a charcoal fire drinking cocktails.

I asked how the Money Islanders got their food and other supplies.

"A launch runs out from Stony Creek every hour between 7 A.M. and 9 P.M. for a dollar the round trip, and its four-o'clock run is what we call the grocery boat," Mr. Coley said. "If we phone the Stony Creek grocery store in the morning, they'll put our order on the four-o'clock boat and it'll be dropped off for us at the dock."

By now, we had completed our tour of the island, which is only a sixth of a mile long, and had returned to the Coleys' house, where we found Mrs. Coley sitting on the porch. I asked her about the housekeeping problems of island life, and she escorted Mike and me inside and showed us the cistern, the pumps, and other facilities of which her husband had spoken. I inquired whether the house was warm enough in winter, and she told me that Money Island is inhabited only during the summer. "Everybody is off by late fall," she said. "That's when the launch stops running. And you couldn't live out here in winter even if you had your own boat. The well freezes, and these houses aren't winterized, and the Sound sometimes gets so full of ice between here and the shore that you can't use a boat."

When we returned to *Merrywend*, I had to get to work, because it was my night to cook. I served a round of drinks, with crackers and cheese spreads, and then Scotch broth, an entrée of canned boiled ham with Dijon mustard, French-sliced beans, potato salad, the remains of a bottle of Bardolino Bolla we had opened last week (it seemed none the worse for having been sloshed around through several storms), and oatmeal cookies and coffee. We ate in the twilight and finished almost in the dark, with the black water lapping gently at our hull, and the islands now remote and invisible except for a scattering of yellow lights in house windows. Growing drowsy, we leaned back on the cockpit cushions, turned on the radio, and listened to a Brandenburg Concerto. I doubt that even the sybarites in the court of Nero knew pleasure more intense than we did this evening.

Thursday, August 22

At 6:30 A.M., there was nothing outside the porthole by my bunk except a cottony whiteness. I stood up in the companionway and looked out the hatch; we seemed to be floating alone in the universe, in the center of a small patch of water that blended into gray-white nothingness twenty yards away. After straining my eyes for a while, I finally saw—or thought I saw—the shadowy silhouette of a sloop that had anchored near us late yesterday afternoon, and, in another direction, several oyster stakes I had noticed on our way in. But fifteen minutes later the fog had thickened, as it sometimes does at dawn, and the sloop and the oyster stakes were gone; *Merrywend* was now lost in a gray, clammy limbo. A motor throbbed somewhere and came closer, running very slowly. It dropped down to idling speed and I could hear voices; then it revved up a bit and moved, unseen, across our stern. The time was 7 A.M., and I concluded that the launch was running on schedule. I felt considerable admiration for the man at the wheel, who on a morning like this could find his way among the islands by compass and timing.

For anyone else, of course, it would have been idiocy to move a boat around in such weather, so after breakfast we waited as patiently as we could for the fog to burn off. It began to thin a little toward 9 A.M.; the light brightened, and we could faintly see the outlines of the islands on either side of us. Although the visibility was only a few hundred feet, we decided we could safely hoist anchor and leave; the passage out from between the islands and through the nearby rocks was well marked, and I could navigate buoy-to-buoy until we reached open water. Thus far on the trip, I had had no need to do any of this kind of navigating, so today presented an opportunity, of sorts. Navigating buoy-to-buoy is not a complex procedure, but it does call for close attention. Starting at any known buoy or position, the navigator consults the chart, finds the distance and the proper compass course to the next buoy, and gives the heading to the helmsman—provided, that is, that the wind will allow the boat to sail that way. If not, it may be necessary to make a series of short tacks, plotting them out on the chart to see where the boat is getting to. Judging the speed through the water from experience, and making due allowance for the effect of the current at the moment, the navigator predicts when the next buoy should appear out of the fog ahead. When it does, and is definitely identified by color, shape, and number, he is ready to name the heading for another buoy. All in all, the process is not unlike feeling one's way to the bathroom at night with closed eyes.

Navigating like this in heavy fog is possible because the Coast Guard has been prodigal in marking Long Island Sound. Every major rock, reef, and shoal, every island or projecting point of land, every harbor and channel has its reference markers in the form of buoys moored strategically nearby, while key landmarks or major hazards have foghorns, sirens, whistles, radio beacons, or lighthouses. In the spring I had visited Coast Guard headquarters in the Custom House and talked with a couple of officers in the Aids to Navigation Branch about buoys and other markers. They told me that Long Island Sound then had thirteen "attended light stations" (Coast Guard terminology for manned lighthouses onshore or offshore), and seventy-five automatic ones. Some of the latter are old lighthouses that have been automated, but most are steel towers with flashing lights mounted on them; the old stone lighthouses, usually nearby, stand vacant and forlorn, deserted by the man-and-wife teams or the Coast Guard crews who used to live in them. Five of the manned lighthouses, in addition to their powerful lights, have radio transmitters, each with its own frequency and Morse Code identification. A mariner lost on the Sound at night or in fog can tune in, say, Falkner Island (a steady tone on 306 kilocycles, periodically interrupted by ·—··, the Morse code symbol for L) on a direction-finding radio; by turning it slowly to get a "null" or complete loss of sound, he can tell in what direction Falkner Island lies. Then, if he does the same with a second radio beacon—perhaps the one at Stratford Shoal (286 kilocycles, with ·——· or P as its identification), he can draw on his chart two lines representing the directions in which the two stations lie, and find his own position by extending the lines until they intersect.

In addition to the manned and unmanned light stations, floating navigational aids are carefully planted around the waters of the Sound. Technically they are all buoys—floating objects chained to "sinkers," blocks of concrete weighing anywhere from five hundred pounds to a ton, which rest on the bottom—but they come in a wide variety of styles to minimize the chance of mistaken identity, and are all numbered for the same reason. There are about a hundred and thirty lighted buoys; the smallest of them are little derricklike structures five feet high, bolted onto air-filled steel floats and having tiny battery-operated flashing lights at their top, and the largest are thirty-two-foot floating towers with brilliant lights, powered by massive batteries. Various types of lighted buoys also have bells or gongs inside the framework of their towers; these automatically toll as waves rock the buoys about and swing their clappers. Some also have whistles, which are high-pitched intermittent horns operated by tanks of compressed air. The most populous category consists of unlighted gongs, bells, whistles, and ordinary nuns and cans, of which there are some five hundred and forty around the Sound; most of them mark channels or act as offshore check points near channels and obstructions.

All these various buoys must be regularly nourished and clothed, and the Coast Guard installations at Eatons Neck and New London have boats and crews assigned to this duty. They visit all the buoys on a regular schedule, revitalizing them with fresh batteries, bulbs, tanks of air, and fuel for their generators. Once a year each buoy is grappled by the crane of a buoy tender and hauled aboard to have its chain and shackles inspected, and to be repainted, since both the salt water and the droppings of sea gulls tend to corrode and obscure the color and the numbers painted on them. The buoys are all marked on the charts with considerable accuracy, and if a storm moves one out of place, that fact is immediately reported in a weekly mimeographed "Local Notice to Mariners," which the Coast Guard mails out at no charge to anyone asking to be on the list; as soon as possible, a buoy tender hoists up the offending buoy and sinker, and drops them back in the water where they are supposed to be. A forty-foot work boat which I had seen at Eatons Neck can handle the smaller ones, but the big floating lights must be dealt with by a hundred-and-eighty-foot work boat based at New London.

Coastguardmen are able to view with equanimity the continual damage done to their buoys by storms, salt water, and the gulls, but they get cranky when the aids are misused by untutored mariners, especially fishermen, who frequently moor their boats to them; this occasionally drags the buoys out of position, and, in any case, it obscures them from other mariners, for which reasons doing so is a federal offense and can result in a fine of from $500 to $2500. Such behavior is part of the widespread ignorance concerning navigational aids which leads many a novice mariner to run hard aground, or to get lost and shout frantically for help on his ship-to-shore radio. Just how many present-day Long Island mariners actually understand the navigational aids and can use them properly is anyone's guess; the guess of the Coast Guard officers I talked to was about 10 per cent.

Happily, we were among that 10 per cent, and at 9:20 A.M. we hoisted anchor and motored slowly down the channel between the islands, on a course of 233° magnetic. About six hundred yards beyond Horse Island, Can 5 appeared thirty or forty yards off our starboard side, as we had expected, and we thereupon altered course ten degrees to the left to avoid a reef lying between Can 5 and Nun 4, as yet unseen. In a little while, both Nun 4 and Can 3, beyond it, were dimly but reassuringly visible; there was a safe passage between them, and we turned to 280° magnetic and went through it, meanwhile hoisting sail and killing the motor. The wind was light, and we estimated our speed under sail at two to three knots; with just a mile to go to Can 1, at Gangway Rock, we expected to be upon it in about twenty minutes, and to see it dead ahead in fifteen. It most gratifyingly appeared right on schedule, and we swung left at once to 228°, which would take us to Branford Reef lighthouse, a mile and a third away. The fog was now dissolving rapidly, though, and when we were still half a mile from the lighthouse we were able to see it. Because our distance from the shore was more than a mile, we felt that it would be quite safe not to travel the full distance to the lighthouse, and, instead, we took up a westward heading that would keep us outside all obstructions and bring us to the mouth of New Haven Harbor in about an hour.

New Haven is the busiest commercial port on Long Island Sound, and has been since the early eighteen-hundreds, when many of its ships cleared for such distant places as China and the South Seas. It is usually shunned by yachtsmen, but I wanted to see what it was like. The tapering harbor is a mile and a half wide at its mouth and three miles deep, and is protected by three stone breakwaters lying well out in the Sound. A broad channel, dredged deep enough for large cargo ships, runs through the breakwaters and up the middle of the harbor to the city. We rounded Morgan Point, on the eastern side of the harbor mouth, at 11 A.M. and started up the harbor proper. Out here near the Sound, all we could see on the shoreline was a public beach, an amusement park, and some private houses, but soon enough there began to appear, along both sides, the grimy, busy world of industry. Well up in the harbor, the east side was a forest of cranes and a sooty jumble of freighters, coal piles, conveyors, smokestacks, and gas tanks, while the west side consisted of railroad yards, factories, and tall office buildings.

At the moment, there were no boats moving around except for one large tug and one freighter, each of which passed us in the channel. At other times of day, or on other days in the week, we might have seen plenty of activity, for some four hundred ocean-going commercial vessels enter the port each year. The most frequently seen cargo vessels are tankers, which bring in various petroleum products, in quantities up to forty-one thousand tons in a single hull. Freighters, in lesser number, haul in various raw and semifinished materials and carry away scrap iron. Tugs, of course, tow in barges loaded with coal, sand, and rock, and sometimes pull them away carrying "spoil," or dredged-up sand and earth, which may be dumped in certain areas of the Sound carefully specified on the charts.

We were now well up the channel, and through the film of haze in the air and the smoke of the city we could see the docks and cargo vessels, the heaped-up water tanks, factories, office buildings, and apartment buildings of the city, and the Connecticut Turnpike, streaking along near the waterfront. The haze and our distance from the city—a mile or so—made everything seem still quite removed and otherworldly, but then, gradually, we became aware of the city in a new way: we heard it. Across the water and all around us there was now the sound of the city's breathing—a deep, pervasive roar, oceanic and yet mechanical, that was a blending of the noises of trains and trucks and buses, machinery and cars, factories and waterfront cranes. Together, they produced a continuous grinding, humming *sostenuto* note—a sound that one is hardly ever conscious of when one is actually in a city.

Having had a close enough look at urban life for the moment, we came about and tacked down the channel. We felt a sense of escape as the muffled din and the stained air receded astern, yet outside the harbor mouth things were not altogether pleasant this day; the air had become increasingly hazy and humid, and the wind was failing. We were indolent and grouchy, and the gulls lined up on the long, bleak breakwaters seemed to share our feelings; instead of flying or gliding, they sat unmoving and stared mindlessly out to sea. Drifting along in the lightest of winds, we fell into a half sleep, until after about three hours we passed Nun 12, off Pond Point, and could see the deep semicircle of Milford Harbor a mile and a half ahead. On the horizon far to our left was a row of ballooning bright-colored spinnakers, so we knew a race was in progress, and as we drew closer to Milford Harbor, the spinnakers rapidly grew larger; they were on 210s—sleek thirty-foot day-sailers—that were returning to Milford Yacht Club, just inside the mouth of the Wepawaug River, at the inner end of the harbor. This being our destination, too, we dropped sail and started up the motor, to let the racing boats troop in before us, still flying their gaily colored spinnakers. When they were all safely inside, we followed them, and were assigned by the dockmaster to a fore-and-aft mooring tucked in close to scores of other pleasure craft and only a dozen yards from a channel in which power cruisers, fishing boats, tugs, and oyster boats were plowing to and fro.

When I first visited Milford by boat, ten years ago, it seemed wonderfully unchanged from older days, and the people at the simple, unpretentious yacht club struck me as unusually friendly and easygoing. The river was pleasantly but not densely cluttered with pleasure boats and oyster dredges; squadrons of brown ducks paddled around, complaining vociferously; a little beach in front of the yacht club was always dotted with children; and bustling about importantly was a denim-clad, red-faced hulk of a man, known to all seasoned Long Island Sound mariners as Captain Bradley, who served both club members and transients as an unofficial nautical factotum and could fix nearly anything in a matter of minutes. But by now, Milford's charm had worn a bit thin. There were too many boats, the water was consequently rather foul, Captain Bradley was on the outs with the yacht club, and since the opening of the Connecticut Turnpike the village had begun turning into just another bedroom town, serving New Haven to the east and Bridgeport to the west. Even so, Mike and Alan and I found it still a fairly pleasant place to be, but I wonder how long it will keep this quality.

We showered in a bathhouse onshore, phoned for a taxi, and had dinner in town. (We had expected to eat at the club, but tonight they were having a special buffet dinner for the crews of the 210s.) After dinner, Mike and Alan went down to the beach and slumped into a couple of deck chairs, and I headed for the club to see what I could see. A couple of hundred sunburned extroverts in sports clothes were eating and talking at a great rate. I asked to meet one of the club's officers, and was soon having coffee with its vice-commodore, Thurston B. Sumner. He explained that the race I had seen this afternoon included representatives of every fleet of 210s entering the national championships—eighteen in all—and that they would be racing again in the morning. Most of the crewmen in this class were young adults, he said, but the Milford Yacht Club had fleets of five other classes of boats—Blue Jays, Lightnings, Thistles, Stars, and Fireflies—which youngsters could manage. "We're probably the most active sailing club in the Sound," he went on. "As you can see, we don't go in much for the fancier side of yacht-club life. This is essentially a racing and family club. I guess that's one of the reasons transients have always considered us friendly rather than snobbish. Only trouble is, nowadays it's got so we just can't handle them all, especially when we have a regatta of our own going on. It's got so that boats that used to moor in here without any difficulty are having to anchor outside in the harbor, in the lee of Charles Island. That isn't any too comfortable in an easterly wind, and the launch can't go way out there for them, but what can we do? Sometimes I wonder what's going to happen to the whole business of boating on the Sound. Things are changing fast, and at the present rate we simply won't be able to be hospitable to visitors. Boating will go the way motoring did, and that will be a sad thing to see."

On this dismal note, we finished our coffee, and said good night. I collected my crew outside, and rowed with them back to *Merrywend* through masses of raucously indignant ducks.

AT MILFORD, the Sound is still seventeen miles wide, but west of there it begins to constrict, and its shoreline becomes ever more densely populated. Since we were now less than thirty miles from Stamford, we would have only one more night on the boat, and we wanted to make the most of our last chance to anchor out and savor the sense of solitude and remoteness now so nearly unobtainable at this end of the Sound. After studying both the charts and the *Cruising Guide*, we decided to try anchoring near Sheffield Island, one of a group of islands lying just south of Norwalk.

This morning, the eastern part of the United States, including Milford, was still covered by a mass of warm, humid southern air. When I awoke, it lay motionless and almost viscid, and fog cloaked the river and harbor. There was nothing to be done until it lifted. I lay in my bunk reading; the stillness was broken only by occasional arguments among Captain Bradley's ducks, but slowly I became aware of another sound —a steady whining or grinding, somewhat like the sound of a distant factory or great piece of machinery. After some reflection, I remembered having heard this sound before in other small Connecticut harbors. It is the basic chord struck by the Turnpike, its component notes being the broiling noise of tires, the roaring of motors, the snarling of truck gears, and the rush of turbulent air. In scores of beach resorts, harbors, and quiet coastal towns where human beings once slept in blessed native silence, there now is never real silence; at every hour of day and night the air is sullied by the seepage of the sound of commerce. Like the stench in an oil-refining town, it becomes tolerable and unnoticeable after a while to the residents, but never to the visitor; cruising boatmen and summer residents are aware of the noise, and at least some of them are filled with regret for the irrecoverable silence of the recent past.

The fog dissipated a little before ten o'clock, but there was still no wind, so we started the motor and eased away from the mooring. The cheerful young men and women coming out to their moored 210s were faced with the prospect of paddling two miles to the bell outside Milford Harbor where the race would begin, and on our way out we picked up a towline and hauled a string of six of them along with us; two other boats using power towed the remainder. When they dropped off at the bell, they hoisted sail and, miraculously, were able to glide around, wringing movement out of the faintest of breezes. Soon it came up a little stronger, and then we, too, hoisted sail and began moving slowly along.

We proceeded southwest, and before long we could see the breakwater outside the mouth of the Housatonic River and, near it, the lighthouse on Stratford Point. Looking north across the marshes on the eastern side of the Housatonic, we could also see the upper part of the American Shakespeare Theatre, two and a half miles away, its teak planking and great frontal diadem unmistakable even through this morning's milky air. Over the past several years, I have arrived by boat three times for performances at the Shakespeare Theatre, and have concluded that this is the most agreeable way imaginable to go to a show. One sails from someplace an easy day's journey away, such as Price Bend, at Huntington Harbor, leaving at 9 A.M., say, and spending the morning and early afternoon crossing the Sound on a long diagonal. Then, if all has gone well, one drops anchor near the breakwater outside the Housatonic and has a good swim, perhaps using salt-water soap first on deck to turn the swim into a bath. Then into clean sports clothes, and upstream using power.

(This river has a current that can reach two and a half knots.) Beyond the Bridgeport municipal airport and the Sikorsky helicopter plant, the river curves around to the right and the theater looms up, handsomely archaic-looking, on the west bank. Just near it on the river are the dock and small white clubhouse of the Housatonic Boat Club, which has very little room for transients but is willing to lend them moorings of members who are out on extended cruises. There are also two boatyards a bit farther upstream, where one can moor if the Boat Club is full. Public relations people of the American Shakespeare Theatre have no accurate idea how many people come to the theater by boat, but have guessed that it is on the order of only a couple of dozen per weekend, plus a smattering during the week.

When I think back on my several boat trips to the theater, a collage of images floats before my eyes, all of them extremely pleasant: mooring the boat near the boat club and having drinks and dinner on board; shaving and dressing in our best (the women on board actually getting into skirts and carrying their high-heeled shoes in hand); rowing to the dock, and sauntering across the theater's broad green lawn, feeling brown and taut and infinitely superior to the soft, white city folk arriving by car from New York. Then the shows themselves—*Midsummer Night's Dream, Antony and Cleopatra, As You Like It;* then walking back across the lawn in the darkness to the dock, while everyone else climbs into cars and roars away on the highway; rowing across the black river toward the pale yellow smudge of light hung on the bow to guide us home; and, finally, sitting in the cockpit on the deserted river, sipping brandy and talking about the play, the audience, the night air, the day's sailing, the luminous plankton in the water, and the marvel of combining physical pleasures with intellectual ones—a process in which the pleasures do not merely add up, but somehow enlarge and heighten each other. J. S. Mill, in his famous criticism of his father's hedonistic calculus, rightly pointed out that pleasures cannot

134

be merely added up, because they differ in quality; but more than that, it almost seems as though the combination of differing kinds of pleasures yields a multiplicative effect. Your true hedonist does not seek to wring ultimate pleasure out of any one form of gratification taken by itself; he knows that simultaneity of dissimilar pleasures is the real connoisseur's way.

The Shakespeare Theatre is a late and atypical aspect of life on the Housatonic. Although narrow, the Housatonic is one of the principal rivers in Connecticut, and as early as 1657 colonists began making the river, far upstream of Stratford, a leading center of shipbuilding. Other shipyards were established downriver later on, and one of them, in Stratford, has been continuously active since 1840, albeit the nature of its clientele has changed several times. In the beginning, the yard turned out great coasting schooners for the lumber and produce trade. This kind of business died out by the end of the century, and in 1896 one William Bedell bought the yard and began to change it and improve it. Known thereafter as Bedell's Shipyard, from the turn of the century on it built and repaired dredgers for the flourishing oyster industry, whose farmers would come from Connecticut harbors and from Huntington Bay and Oyster Bay across the Sound. Early this past summer I had dropped in on Mrs. Betsy Bedell, wife of one of the two grandsons of William Bedell who operate the yard today,* to learn how things were going nowadays. "The starfish have been killing off the oyster industry since the end of the war," she said, "and besides, they use big mechanized boats we can't handle here. We're practically out of that side of the shipyard business. Nowadays we build and repair pleasure boats, and run a marina service for regular customers and for transients. That's how things have changed. But it's a wonderful business to be in, and we love it. We live in that house," she said, waving at a white frame building not far from the dock we were standing on, "and during sum-

* Since my trip, however, the Bedells have sold out to another marina.

mer weekends at least one of us is on the dock from sunup till late at night. The people we serve are mostly our regular customers and friends, and each one has something different he needs or wants taken care of. They turn to us, and we help them. The Sound is changing, and that's the way things are going."

Boat servicing and Shakespeare are the small-scale activities in the lower Housatonic; the large-scale one is the building of helicopters at the Sikorsky plant. Even out on the Sound this morning, we were aware of it, for as we sailed past Stratford Point two helicopters hung five hundred feet or so over the water about a mile offshore, while a third one hovered only fifty feet over the water for a while, then settled onto the surface, swiveled around, lifted off and moved forward a little, and then settled back again, attended all the while by a high-powered motor launch named *Researcher*, which practically vibrated with iridescent orange paint. Vice-Commodore Sumner of the Milford Yacht Club works at Sikorsky, and he had told me the previous evening that these helicopters, which I had seen performing their strange gyrations earlier in the summer, were simply going through a set pattern of tests before delivery, and that *Researcher* stands by during these tests as a crash boat.

Half a mile beyond Stratford Point, the wind failed completely, leaving us motionless on a dead-calm sea. For a time, we tried to wait patiently, like good sailors, for the wind to return, but we sweltered in the sticky heat, and we were tormented by flies that came swarming over the water to join us, so presently we started up the motor and plowed ahead, the breeze of our movement cooling us off and carrying away some of our unwanted guests. Later on, we dropped and furled the sails, and we made no further effort to use them today. Our course took us past the looming smoky ugliness of Bridgeport, the spacious and handsome estates around Black Rock Harbor, the closely packed hip-roofed clapboard houses of Pine Creek Point, and, finally, the waterfront mansions near

Southport, whose church spires we could see a short way inland.

Then the Norwalk Islands appeared ahead, green and low-lying, and scattered more widely than the Thimbles. The Norwalk Islands—there are sixteen of them, not counting mere rocks—are strung out in a line some five miles long and more or less parallel to the irregular shoreline, and about half a mile out from it. The broad sheet of water between the islands and the mainland is, like so many other harbor areas in the Sound, both tempting and treacherous; much of it is only a foot or two deep at low tide, and the parts that are deeper than that are liberally sprinkled with rocks and sand bars just barely covered at middle or high tide. Any stranger entering these waters in the days before charts either was in trouble almost at once or had to proceed at dead slow, taking soundings constantly. Accordingly, the Norwalk Islands were a rallying point during the Revolutionary War for Continental whale-boat crews, who were at home in their waters, and who made forays out into the Sound now and again to attack British boats, which could not easily pursue them when they retreated to their fastness. Despite the shallow and hazardous character of Cockenoe Island Harbor and Sheffield Island Harbor, as the stretch of water between the islands and the mainland is called, there is an excellently marked channel leading through it, most of which is as straight as Fifth Avenue. Midway along the channel, in fact, there is the best landmark for twenty miles along the Connecticut coast—a tremendous smokestack towering over a large, modern-style blue-green power plant, which provides electricity for Norwalk, South Norwalk, and adjacent areas. The channel serves not only pleasure boats but the power plant, and even before we had got fairly into it, a large, dark tug named *M. & J. Tracy* chugged past us towing a heavily loaded coal barge up to the plant's unloading area, where a crane proceeded to bite off great mouthfuls of its coal and spit them out in a black heap on the shore.

Watching our chart closely, we made our way between various lighthouses and buoys in a winding part of the channel. This took us past Cockenoe Island and Goose Island, the former a rather bleak piece of grass-covered flatland and the latter a mere sandspit. The other islands looked a little more appealing; from the channel, we could not make out all the details of their terrain, but we could tell that some were grassy hillocks with a few trees strewn around, while others were larger and were occupied by wooden houses, some landscaping, cabañas, and umbrellas. The channel itself was not very busy this afternoon, but in the shallow waters outside it small powerboats were zipping around, and a few day-sailers were trying to make some headway, despite the lack of wind. To our right loomed the massive power plant, which had lights gleaming from some of its windows and a plume of brownish smoke rising almost straight upward from its stack. Ahead of us and to our left, at the far end of the channel, lay Sheffield Island, overgrown and apparently uninhabited, and with fairly deep and reasonably sheltered water on its north side, which, we felt, would be far enough from the channel, with its power station, and also from the mainland to give us the illusion of remoteness we sought. We dropped anchor near Sheffield Island at 4:30 P.M., reveling in our aloneness. We were, of course, alone only in a relative sense; there was an immense ketch anchored half a mile farther along the shore of Sheffield Island, and a power cruiser a quarter mile off the other way. The ketch was big enough to have a good-sized power launch slung in davits; shortly, this was lowered to the water, and a party of people descended a gangway from the big boat to the launch and motored away. We looked up the boat—*Wayfarer*, of New York—and found that the companion of our anchorage belonged to Laurance S. Rockefeller and David Rockefeller. We were impressed.

The evening was a kind of farewell performance, in which we tried to recapitulate the best things we had done on board during the week: we swam, shaved with hot water, and put on clean clothes for our own pleasure, even though there were no women on board; drank numerous martinis and uttered a great deal of platitudinous philosophic talk about pleasure, work, and the brevity of life; speculated idly about life on the nearby islands, especially tiny Tavern Island a third of a mile across the channel from us, on whose several acres we could make out formal stairways, a Tudor mansion, and dozens of statues along the stone balustrades and on the manicured lawn (I had been told, earlier in the season, that this minuscule fief is owned by Billy Rose); made an excellent dinner, if one can judge a dinner after four large drinks; and indulged in some foolishness, vague in memory, which involved accidentally dropping the boathook overboard, and leaping in, fully clothed, to retrieve it. Finally, late in the evening, noticing our own tendency to lurch about rather than walk properly, we struck up a bellowing rendition of an old sea chanty, for which I excuse us by reminding myself that it was, after all, Friday night, when Americans traditionally make damned fools of themselves. For the benefit of the Rockefellers, the nearby power cruiser, and any nighttime traffic passing by in the channel, we roared:

> What'll we do with a drunken sailor?
> What'll we do with a drunken sailor?
> What'll we do with a drunken sailor?
>   Earl-eye in the morning?
>
> Heave 'im in the scuppers till he's sober,
> Heave 'im in the scuppers till he's sober,
> Heave 'im in the scuppers till he's sober,
>   Earl-eye in the morning.

And so to bed.

This was the last day of my circumnavigation (if one can be said to circumnavigate a body of water) of Long Island Sound. Another weekend was starting, but the day was one to delight only the hardier variety of sailor. At 7 A.M., the sky was dull gray with swollen clouds, and a crisp, chilly wind was blowing from the west and beginning to vex the surface of the water. Stamford Yacht Haven, our home base and terminus, was only eight and a half miles away, and I had thought we might spend some time poking into interesting places en route. We might have anchored for lunch in Ziegler Cove, a diminutive inlet between Hay Island and Great Island, near Noroton, that is surrounded on nearly all sides by rocks, seawalls, trees, and glimpses of flowing lawns and fine houses. We might have seen the nuns at the Convent of the Sacred Heart on Long Neck Point leaping nimbly about their tennis court in full habit—a sight that had cheered me in the past. We might have sailed up the channel into Westcott Cove, on the eastern side of Shippan Point, to see from offshore the beaches of Stamford where I had been swimming day after day all through the early part of this summer. But such marine tourism calls for a gentle, sun-drenched day. Today was made for fast open-water sailing, and since we'd had no wind at all yesterday, the chance for one last fling was really quite welcome. After hoisting sail and getting our anchor aboard at 9:30 A.M., we tacked close-hauled past the tip of Sheffield Island and a shoal extending beyond it; then we turned south, passing close by Greens Ledge Light and starting a straight, fast reach across the Sound—a seven-mile straight leg to Eatons Neck and past it into Huntington Bay, where I had been eleven days ago. There we would come about and head diagonally back across the Sound toward Stamford Harbor and home.

The air was full of a faint drizzle that cut visibility to a mile or so, but the wind was strong and steady, and we raced along, heeled over handsomely and every so often kicking up a sheet of spray from the choppy waves. Bundled up in sweaters and foul-weather gear, we felt both comfortable and a trifle adventurous, and considered it a marvelous day. All up and down the Sound, on the other hand, would-be sun bathers and swimmers were chafing indoors, peering out the window every few minutes and snarling at the children underfoot, while weekend guests strained to pretend that they were having a fine time despite the weather. Though we were actually close to the Sound's boating center of gravity, we seemed alone this morning. There had been a few fishing boats huddled near the lighthouse, but out in the middle of the Sound, at ten-thirty on an August Saturday morning, there was no one at all to be seen until a large shape appeared off our port bow. This turned out to be the tug *Aquidneck* doggedly shoving a huge, square dredging barge in the direction of New York. We made our landfall at 11 A.M., when we detected, ahead and slightly to the left, the faint shape of a hilly point of land; through the binoculars we could see on it the buildings of the Eatons Neck Coast Guard Station. To the right of it, in Huntington Bay, a few hardy souls were now venturing out in sailboats and powerboats. In another fifteen minutes, we were racing down the bay among them, having skimmed clear across the Sound in an hour and a quarter.

Near Price Bend, we came about and took up a north-northwest heading for Stamford. On this course, we were sailing closer to the wind, and therefore heeling still more. *Merrywend* is a "stiff" boat—one that does not heel over much from the pressure of the wind in her sails—but this particular morning we took delight in sailing her hard and sheeted in close, so as to get her rail under and make foaming green water rush along the leeward deck amidships. Having been on board for days, we were at ease with even this much heeling, and enjoyed our sense of mastery over wind and water, which is one of the special pleasures men can get from Long Island Sound, and one of the reasons they cherish it. This crossing took longer, but it was even more exhilarating than the first one. Spray lashed us and ran down our faces, and we laughed and took turns walking forward—hanging onto shrouds and stays all the time—to stand on the bow and feel the powerful lunge and soar of the boat.

Toward 1 P.M., as the Stamford lighthouse and twin breakwaters became visible about a mile ahead, an ugly slate-blue squall line appeared in the west and moved toward us rapidly. My trip had been unusual in that I had not yet been caught by a storm except at anchor; in other summers I had sailed through a number of storms during a one- or two-week cruise. Sailing through a storm on the Sound is an exciting experience. The wind picks up in a matter of minutes, and almost at once the sea starts to heave and surge, whereupon the boat, pounding up and down, seems to lose much of her ability to move forward; moreover, the rudder becomes slow to respond, and one has to crank the wheel far around one way and then the other to keep her headed properly. Sheets of water leap up and smack onto the deck and into the cockpit, lightning splits the sky, and thunder shatters the air. Then, finally, the rain slashes down violently, and in an instant visibility is reduced to a hundred feet or so; the helmsman steers by compass, unsure of where he is on the chart but too busy keeping the boat from broaching even to look. With luck, no barges or rocks loom up dead ahead in the thick curtain of rain, and in fifteen or twenty minutes the rain abruptly slacks off, the wind drops, the visibility picks up to a quarter or half mile, and one realizes all at once that one will come through alive and undamaged. Then, after perhaps half an hour more, the mass of clouds is gone and the sun appears, the wet clothes come off, the shivering stops, the boat slides easily over the gentling sea, and all on board agree that it has been marvelous.

We were not to get a full measure of delight today, however. The center of the storm passed us about a mile to the south, and we got only its fringe. Even so, the lee rail was continuously under water, the boat was thumping against the tumbling waves, and a light rain was stinging our eyes. We boiled on through the opening between the breakwaters, and were in Stamford Harbor. Immediately, the water was smooth, and even the wind quickly moderated. As we sailed farther up the harbor and into the lee of the land, everything became mild and gentle; we could appreciate as land-bound human beings never do the real import of the word "harbor." And by the time we had dropped sail and started up the motor, the sun was breaking through, adding the ultimate touch of warmth and tranquillity to our sense of being harbored and home.

We chugged up the narrow channel of East Branch and around a breakwater toward Pier 5 in Yacht Haven, where *Merrywend* is berthed. I slowly eased her into her slip, and Mike and Alan leaped onto the dock with mooring lines and made her fast; it was just 2 P.M. when I cut the motor, and the trip was over. The moment the boat was secure, we realized that we had forgotten to eat lunch during our last ride; we therefore hauled out all the leftover cold cuts, cheese, bread, butter, tomatoes, and cold beer, and ate ravenously, sitting in the sunny cockpit. After lunch, we put the boat in order, scrubbing her inside and out, stowing winch handles and other removable gear below, emptying the icebox, rearranging the charts, and packing our own clothing.

At last, everything was done, and we locked the companionway hatch, shouldered our duffelbags, and stepped off *Merrywend* onto the dock. We walked along the dock and up to an adjacent parking lot, where we paused to look back once at the graceful white boat, at the blue harbor lying beyond Yacht Haven, and at the Sound beyond that—already another world to us. Our feet were on land, the car door was open, and a different life was reasserting itself. We turned our backs on the water, climbed into the car, and drove away.